FLOWERING SHRUBS AND SMALL TREES

BOOKS BY JEAN HERSEY

Halfway to Heaven
I Like Gardening
Garden in Your Window
Carefree Gardening
Wild Flowers to Know and Grow
The Woman's Day Book of House Plants
A Sense of Seasons
The Shape of a Year
Cooking with Herbs
Flowering Shrubs and Small Trees

WITH ROBERT HERSEY

These Rich Years
Change in the Wind

Flowering Shrubs and Small Trees

One Hundred and Sixty Nine Varieties for Your Garden

JEAN HERSEY

Illustrated by Allianora Rosse

CHARLES SCRIBNER'S SONS · NEW YORK

1 3 5 7 9 11 13 15 17 19 MD/C 20 18 16 14 12 10 8 6 4 2

Printed in the United States of America
Library of Congress Catalog Card Number 73-18299
ISBN 0-684-13701-1

For Banks and Tracy whose sense of wonder,
appreciation of beauty and love of all that grows
is a continual inspiration.

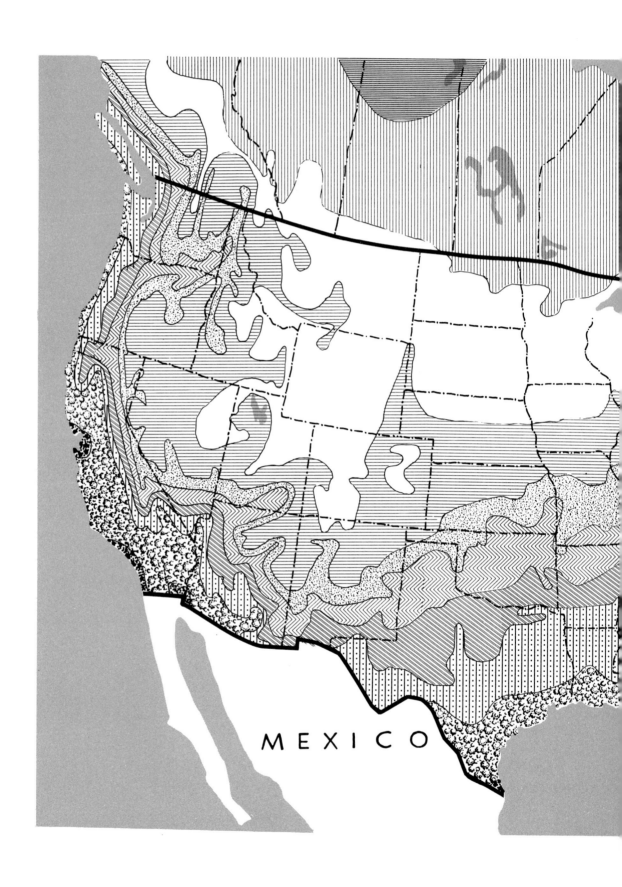

MEXICO

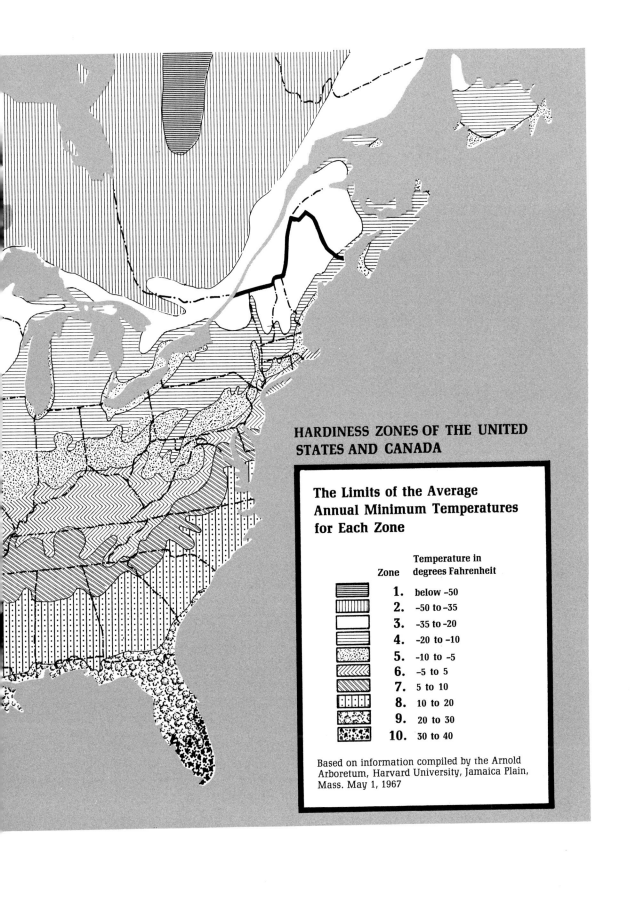

HARDINESS ZONES OF THE UNITED STATES AND CANADA

The Limits of the Average Annual Minimum Temperatures for Each Zone

Zone	Temperature in degrees Fahrenheit
1.	below –50
2.	–50 to –35
3.	–35 to –20
4.	–20 to –10
5.	–10 to –5
6.	–5 to 5
7.	5 to 10
8.	10 to 20
9.	20 to 30
10.	30 to 40

Based on information compiled by the Arnold Arboretum, Harvard University, Jamaica Plain, Mass. May 1, 1967

Contents

Foreword

Introduction   3

Spring Flowering   11

Summer Flowering   49

Fall Flowering   71

Winter Flowering   75

Bibliography   78

Index   80

Foreword

Our horticultural predecessors have assembled in America, for our choice, plants from Europe and Asia to add to selections of native plants of North America. Surprisingly few plants from South America, Africa or Australia grace our outdoor gardens since their climatic requirements are found in but few areas of the United States. While we have a great choice, we still have much to learn about the tolerances of individual plants. Hardiness zones, as given in this book, have become standard generalized designations of where a plant will grow, excluding micro-climatic niches, yet horticulturists offer only the cold end of the hardiness range. In many areas the summer heat or lack of rain, or the nature of the onset of winter, or the frequency of late spring frosts may be more important for the survival of the plant than the extent of winter cold. We cannot recommend the warm end of the hardiness zone, either for practical reasons, or because we often do not know. A plant which requires a long warm season to flower may well survive a northern winter but lack the time to flower or set fruits as you wish. In contrast, many shrubs or fruit trees which do well in a northern area would not be recommended for a southern zone, for while they may live they may lack the cold period essential for the production of flowers.

The oft quoted "plan before planting" might better be "plan before buying" as this volume will indicate to you. Why do you want a particular plant? The reason for your choice might be the spring flowers, sweet scent, fall foliage, attractive fruit, winter bark color, its use as a screen or shade, or for cutting or drying, or any combination of these or other reasons. Now, where do you want it? Should your plant stand alone, be in a combination, be at the front of a flower bed or at the back, be next to the house, or near a walk or driveway? A good plant can be in a wrong location from your point of view or for its own success. Consider your garden during all seasons and plant for each. Consider, also, its appearance next year and ten years hence and choose your plants accordingly. Plants can be moved or propagated but why plant now so that such action is necessary later?

In general, the young plant you choose for your garden should be pampered for the first few years. Once established a tree or shrub will generally endure greater extremes of weather, or neglect, than the new one. The early care you supply protects your investment and enhances your enjoyment of the ultimate success of your planting.

Finally, the plant you choose has a name and the nursery who sold it or the friend who gave it should know what it is called. Save that name. Permanent labels are often available or you can prepare a label to attach to the plant, or, in any case, whrite the name where you can find it again. How satisfying it is to both parties when the question "what is it" can be answered accurately. Share the beauty you grow by knowing the name of your plant.

The pages that follow contain much information on some excellent trees and shrubs. May you find this book useful and enjoyable.

RICHARD A. HOWARD
The Arnold Arboretum of Harvard University
Jamaica Plain, Massachusetts

Introduction

Have you ever stood beside a star magnolia in April while the spring sun streamed down and each flower seemed made of crisp shiny white satin ribbon? When you were little did you ever fill a May basket with pink weigela blooms for your favorite aunt? Such moments of spring enchantment also include looking up through the branches of a blossoming pink dogwood to the blue sky; reading in the hammock while the scent of mock orange wafts your way; and a high point, of course, is the time the child in your life brings you a Mother's Day bouquet of sweet scented viburnum, lavender lilacs, or honeysuckle.

If you live in the South surely you have paused beneath a jacaranda tree in a falling snow of violet petals. Perhaps you have been captured by the sheer beauty of foaming masses of golden acacia tumbling over feathery gray-green foliage, or the sound of a mocking bird trilling his melody from the topmost branch of a paulownia tree in full bloom. Haven't you at some time tucked a mahogany colored blossom of the strawberry shrub into your purse and carried the fruity scent with you all day?

Who isn't stirred by the late New England winter sunlight on silver pussy willow branches, each one with its gay promise of spring? Who hasn't gasped at the beauty of a bank of spungold forsythia, or the delicate Shadblow, a shimmering mist of snowy whiteness in the early spring scene? Step under a flowering fruit—a peach, a crabapple, or a cherry when the branches are blossom laden and listen to the humming of bees. You will return to this busy hurrying world refreshed from these few moments in fairyland.

The excitement and joys of flowering shrubs and small flowering trees move through every season. The spring show merges into a summer display. Watch the butterflies drift and hover over a full flowering buddleia bush. A Rose of Sharon is a delight in the garden. And a single flower is for floating in a graceful, low bowl on the dining table. There is also, for appreciation, the formal splendor of great hydrangeas in a summer seashore garden. The color of the sea surely has splashed up to tint these huge blue heads of bloom.

In autumn Nature goes riotously mad and flings all her colors about. Some of the most vivid shades fall on the berries of the firethorn, the cotoneaster, the barberry, and the rugosa rose "hips." Who can say which are the most magnificently brilliant—these berried shrubs in your garden or the red and yellow maples overhead.

There are so many reasons for planting flowering shrubs and trees. We grow them for their beauty and fragrance in the garden, and for armfuls of flowers to pick for indoors. We grow them because many are easy and carefree, and because we happen to like them.

From a practical angle, flowering shrubs and trees have many uses. Certain ones make wonderful screen plantings. They enclose a garden area for privacy with a wall of living green and colorful blossoms. There are varieties to create an appropriate background for perennials, a cover for steep banks, or gradual slopes. Some make attractive unclipped hedges—a lilac hedge is a sensation, and so is one of the Rose of Sharon bushes. Still other shrubs and trees form a graceful boundary line on your land. An individual shrub growing alone provides not only a decorative feature, a color accent, but all by itself, in its flowering season, it becomes a bouquet in your garden. Best of all, flowering shrubs last weeks in bloom. By selecting proper sorts for your particular climate you can have a sucession of blossoms all summer, and all year if you live in the South. Aside from its beauty and charm and numerous uses in landscaping, this plant material comes trailing with delightful lore and legend from its far away and distant past.

A large number originally came to us from across the sea. Lilacs grew many, many years ago in Arabia and Persia. From here they were brought to English gardens. The popular song that used to be on every old-time hand organ is still occasionally heard today.

> Come down to Kew in lilac-time,
>   in lilac-time, in lilac-time;
> Come down to Kew in lilac-time . . .
> And you shall wander hand in hand
>   with love in summer's wonderland . . .

It was the seventeenth century when the common purple lilac was first brought across the Atlantic to a New England garden. Later on, the white ones came. From Scotland we hear a charming lilac story about a wee Scotch child named Flora who had a brand new dress and wanted so very much to wear it to a party. Her mother always consulted the lilac outside the door to see if it was going to rain. And of course the dress mustn't get wet. In that area, if the lilac leaves dripped water from the mist, rain was imminent. If not, it would clear. Flora secretly ran out ahead of her mother and shook off the misty drops. When her mother consulted her favorite weather oracle, no drops remained, and all looked auspicious for the weather and the new dress. Of course, so runs the tale, the rain descended in torrents, and Flora returned from the party, a wetter, and we trust a wiser child.

In southern Europe the mock orange grows wild, and from that part of the world comes an enchanting legend of how this bush first came into being. Two wood nymphs were dancing in the forest. Badly frightened by the sudden appearance of Pan and Bacchus, they fled only to be blocked by a wide stream. They called on the water nymphs to save them. The God of the River changed one into a reed and the other into a sheltering bush above it. Pan, not to be thwarted, seized the reed, put it to his lips and found to his surprise that by blowing through it he could produce hauntingly sweet music. The pipes of Pan were ever after made from reeds. Bacchus, not to be outdone, broke off a stalk of the mock orange. To create a sound, however, he found he must put a hole in the stem and remove the pith. When he did this he had a clear-toned whistle. In certain European countries today the mock orange is still called the "Whistle Tree."

In the days of ancient Greece the brides of Athens carried boughs of hawthorn to the altar of Hymen, the God of Marriage. The ceremony itself was lit by torches of flaming hawthorn. When a small baby arrived, a few green leaves of this bush were placed in the crib. Hawthorn was the emblem of hope, and in the hearts of each bridal pair in every era and every country, lie hopes of home, children, long lives together, and a growing richness of relationships. No wonder this tree with its special significance was so prominent at weddings.

As well as giving us pleasant tales to think about, and bringing us beauty and filling many garden needs, a flowering tree or bush, once planted, is apt to be with you for years, maybe even for a lifetime, or for several generations. Assuming that you provide proper soil and location, it will grow larger and healthier each season. A simple garden composed solely of these plants is among the most appealing as well as the most carefree of all to grow. Annually, each variety brings you a mass of blooms and often fragrance. In summer, birds nest in these shrubs and small trees. Robins and catbirds are especially partial to lilacs as a place to rear a family. Hummingbirds saddle their nests on a horizontal apple tree branch while a pair of goldfinches settle in the bayberry. When their blossoms pass, the foliage and general appearance of these shrubs and trees contribute delightfully to the outdoor scene. Even after the leaves have dropped, the bare branch form has particular charm in the winter landscape. In cold weather, protecting thickets are vital to all birds. Here they find shelter from storms and wind. What a secure thicket is formed by these bushes and trees.

It is a particular joy in late winter to trim off and bring in boughs of certain shrubs which will flower weeks ahead of their outdoor season. Forsythia presents its sunny splendor to your living room in January. (If you let the blossoms fall and small leaves develop, and give it fresh water occasionally, rootlets form and by spring you've a new bush or two or six to plant outside.) Lilacs flower indoors, but with miniature blooms, and seldom in color. Even a deep lavender lilac will most likely open a white blossom in the house. Most fruit trees will unfold their blooms inside well ahead of spring. We have brought in dogwood branches which winter gales had broken off—for we would never pick them otherwise—and have had a veritable flower show.

Generally all this plant material fares best when set out in early spring or fall when dormant or nearly so. The most important rule and perhaps the basic one is: select the proper variety for your particular soil, and exposure, or else create the needed environment. It is much easier and more satisfactory all around to grow what likes your particular land.

When setting out the newly selected shrub or tree, give it plenty of root room. Dig a large hole, loosen the earth in the bottom so that young rootlets have plenty of soft soil to spread and grow in. Soak these roots as you plant and afterwards. Leave little "dikes" of soil for a few weeks around each plant to hold water. Bushes that are set out in the early spring need much less watering, and if set out in New England in March almost none at all. The spring rains save you carrying many a pailful. A late-planted shrub will have to be watered for several weeks and in dry spells all that first summer.

Where winters are mild a fall planting is successful. But in our North Carolina area we've had better luck with shrubs set out in February. In both spring and autumn local nurseries sell small-sized shrubs and young trees with balled roots. Sometimes these transplant more readily than the ones with bare roots, especially if spring has come in a rush and caught you unawares. If you are behind in your gardening and are setting things out later than usual, try to find material with balled roots.

There is little or no care involved in successfully growing flowering shrubs. Prune them to keep them shapely and remove old tough wood. Open out the centers to let in light and air for certain varieties such as forsythia, mock orange, and weigela. With the center uncluttered there will be more blossoms. Most flowering trees need no pruning at all. Both trees and shrubs usually benefit from a little food before their time of bloom. Thereafter, fertilize every year or so to keep an abundance of good-sized flowers.

Flowering shrubs are enhanced by certain spring bulbs growing with them as companions. A few of our favorite combinations include blue grape hyacinths and crocuses beneath star magnolia; blue grape hyacinths under *Viburnum Carlesii;* forsythia underplanted with blue *chionodoxa, Scilla siberica,* or grape hyacinths. Some of the early botanical tulips such as the *Kaufmanniana* hybrids, and the "White Emperor" tulips are fine companions to forsythia. Set out all these bulbs in the fall.

What an assortment of irresistible flowering shrubs and small trees we have to choose from. They add to the pleasures of gardening in innumerable ways. Somewhere in your outdoors, surely, there is a place just waiting for at least one flowering shrub or small flowering tree. You might even have an urge to create a whole garden of this intriguing plant material. Each year that these bushes inhabit your area they grow more attractive. Once you get to know them and grow them, great fun awaits you and the rewards are endless.

On some brisk spring or fall day, while planting your new bare branched bushes or trees, you will probably find yourself doing what every gardener does. Those of us who love the soil and love working with it stretch our perceptions to include not only the present but to take in the past and the future also. While you dig and plant the shrub of the moment, you remember how it appeared when you saw it in flower in a garden somewhere, or in the pages of a catalogue. Tucking the earth in among the roots with your hands and shovelling more dirt about, watering, and giving it the final touches, you visualize how it will look blossoming. You may even step ahead a few years and in your mind's eye see it quite large. Every gardener knows the excitement of living in many seasons at once, of standing with feet firmly in the now, but also touching lightly and joyously both the past and the future.

Spring Flowering

1. ABELIA-LEAF, KOREAN
(*Abeliophyllum distichum*)

Height: 3–4 ft.
Deciduous
Season of Flowering: early Spring
Fragrant
Location: full sun
Soil: average
Propagation: softwood cuttings
Zone 5, maybe 6, and 4 if sheltered

Purple buds visible in the fall. Starry white spring flowers are followed by blue-green foliage. Arching branches give a graceful open effect. Protect from north and west winds. Sometimes called White Forsythia.

2. ALMOND, FLOWERING
(*Prunus glandulosa*)

Height: 4 ft.
Deciduous
Season of Flowering: Spring
Location: full sun
Soil: average
Propagation: seeds, budding or grafting
Zone 5, maybe 6, 4 if sheltered

Tumbled masses of double flowers like pink or white feathery balls hide stalks. Satiny green leaves follow. Remove any new shoots below graft. Legend says this bush will thrive especially in the garden of a happy and prosperous family. In France it is the symbol of a good marriage.

3. ANDROMEDA, JAPANESE
(*Pieris japonica*)

Height: 5–8 ft.
Evergreen
Season of Flowering: Early Spring
Location: light shade
Soil: acid, rich loam
Propagation: seed, hardwood or softwood
   cuttings
Zone 5, 4 if sheltered

Shell pink buds in trailing pendulous clusters open white showy tassels almost concealing the bush for weeks. Among the earliest of all to bloom. Next year's flower buds form in fall and are attractive all winter. Give ample humus. Don't crowd.

4. APRICOT
(*Prunus armeniaca*)

Height: to 15 ft.
Deciduous
Season of Flowering: Spring
Fruit is edible
Location: full sun
Soil: average
Propagation: budding or grafting, seeds
Zone 7

A beautiful small tree particularly delightful twice a year—when in blossom, and when in fruit. A single tree becomes a huge bouquet of flowers in Spring. Ripening home-grown apricots are a joy for weeks. Eat them fresh from the tree, in jam, cooked, and in countless other ways.

5. AZALEA, CHINESE
(*Rhododendron molle*)

Height: 3–4 ft.
Deciduous
Season of Flowering: Spring
Location: light shade
Soil: acid, rich loam
Propagation: softwood cuttings
Zone 6

Give cool moist soil and leaf mold. Roots easily from early summer cuttings of new wood. Watch for huge night-flying moths that visit yellow flowers for nectar after dark.

6. AZALEA, JAPANESE
(*Rhododendron japonicum*)

Height: 6 ft.
Deciduous
Season of Flowering: Spring
Location: light shade
Soil: acid, rich loam
Propagation: seed or softwood cuttings
Zone 5

Flowers in brilliant tones of red, yellow, or orange. Increases readily not only from cuttings but from your own seed. Sow in the fall in shredded Sphagnum in flats. Set at north window in a temperature of 60°F.

7. AZALEA, KOREAN
(*Rhododendron mucronulatum*)

Height: to 5 ft.
Deciduous
Season of Flowering: Spring
Color: colorful fall leaves
Location: light shade
Soil: adaptable–acid, neutral, but always
   rich loam
Propagation: softwood cuttings
Zone 4

Rosy-purple flowers cover the bush before the last snow melts. Among the earliest. Colorful yellow, bronze, or red leaves enhance the fall scene. This variety withstands a drier soil than other azaleas.

8. AZALEA, PINXTER
(*Rhododendron nudiflorum*)

Height: to 5 ft.
Deciduous
Season of Flowering: Spring
Fragrant
Location: light shade
Soil: acid, rich loam
Propagation: seed or softwood cuttings
Zone 4

Mulch with oak leaves. Naturalize in light, high shade. Boughs of soft, feathery, white and pink blossoms gathered by young people in old New York to decorate for an annual Dutch Pentecostal celebration, Pinxter Frolics. Hence flowers often called Pinxterbloom.

9. BARBERRY
(*Berberis thunbergii*)

Height: 3–6 ft.
Deciduous
Season of Flowering: Spring
Colorful fruit
Colorful autumn leaves and bright red berries
Location: full sun, light shade
Soil: average
Propagation: softwood cuttings, seeds
Zone 4

Compact and an excellent hedge plant (set 2 ft. apart). Can be shaped by pruning as desired. Small yellow and red flowers. Shiny leaves turn deep red in fall and countless showy scarlet berries appear on spiny branches. The roots and bark were used by the ancients medicinally.

10. BARBERRY, COMMON
(*Berberis vulgaris*)

Height: to 6 ft.
Deciduous
Season of Flowering: Spring
Fragrant
Colorful foliage in autumn and bright red berries
Location: full sun, light shade
Soil: average
Propagation: softwood cuttings, seed
Zone 4

In spring the fragrance of hanging yellow flowers greets you on a light breeze. In olden days the leaves were used in salad and to flavor roast goose. Listed in old herbals as a charm against witches.

11. BEACH PLUM
(*Prunus maritima*)

Height: to 10 ft.
Deciduous
Season of Flowering: Spring
Fruit: blue purple
Colorful foliage
Fragrant
Location: full sun or light shade
Soil: acid and light sandy
Propagation: seeds or grafting

Zone 4

Clusters of enchanting, feathery, white flowers adorn the branches in May. Thrives at seashore in almost pure sand. Holds banks. Purple berries in August make delicious jam and jelly.

12. BLUEBERRY, HIGHBUSH
(*Vaccinium corymbosum*)

Height: to 10 ft.
Deciduous
Season of Flowering: Spring
Delicious fruit
Colorful foliage in autumn and berries
Location: full sun
Soil: acid, light sandy
Propagation: softwood cuttings, seeds
Zone 3

Spring branches strung with waxy pink blossoms, each shaped like a miniature Greek urn. Berries in July. Tolerates boggy conditions and dry areas also. Twigs red all winter. Many bright red autumn leaves hold on for months.

13. BROOM, SCOTCH
(*Cytisus scoparius*)

Height: 4–6 ft.
Evergreen
Season of Flowering: Spring
Colorful foliage in fall
Location: full sun, light shade
Soil: light sandy
Propagation: hardwood cuttings
Zone 5

Pea-shaped golden flowers open deep in the heart of the bush. Thrives in dry, sandy, seashore gardens. Evergreen stems attractive in winter snows. Naturalized in New England. Flourishes near pines. Bind the twigs tight together for a home-made hearth brush.

14. BROOM, WARMINSTER
(*Cytisus praecox*)

Height: 4–6 ft.
Evergreen
Season of Flowering: Spring
Colorful foliage in fall
Location: full sun
Soil: light sandy
Propagation: hardwood cuttings
Zone 5

Arching fountain-like branches covered with deeply scented lemon yellow flowers. Makes a fine informal hedge. Twigs green all winter. Tolerates dry sandy soil.

15. BUTTERFLY-BUSH, FOUNTAIN
(*Buddleia alternifolia*)

Height: to 8 ft.
Deciduous
Season of Flowering: Spring
Fragrant flowers
Location: full sun
Soil: average
Propagation: softwood cuttings
Zone 5

Deeply scented lilac flowers on arching branches. On sunny days host to myriads of butterflies. Willow-like leaves. Needs area ten feet square for spreading. Thrives in dry spots. Makes beautiful house bouquets. Prune only after flowering.

16. CALIFORNIA-LILAC
(*Ceanothus purpureus*)

Height: 4 ft.
Evergreen
Season of Flowering: Spring
Colorful branches in winter
Location: full sun
Soil: average
Propagation: hardwood or softwood cuttings
Zone 7

Clusters of dark blue flowers all but hide the foilage. Blooms long lasting in bouquets. Adapts to poor soil and drought. Arching spreading branches attractively red all year.

17. CHERRY, DOUBLE WHITE FLOWERING
(*Prunus serrulata 'Shirofugen'*)

Height: to 15 ft.
Deciduous
Season of Flowering: Spring
Fragrant flowers
Location: full sun
Soil: average
Propagation: softwood cuttings, budding or
  grafting
Zone 7

Spreading habit. Before foliage delicate pink buds open to clouds of pure white flowers. Bronze-green leaves. In Japan people plan "cherry blossom viewing parties." All admire, and often silently.

18. CHERRY-LAUREL
(*Prunus laurocerasus*)

Height: 6–18 ft.
Evergreen
Season of Flowering: Spring
Fruit
Fragrant
Location: full sun, light shade
Soil: rich loam
Propagation: softwood cuttings·
Zone 7

Fragrant white "bottle brush" flowers. In late summer showy, purple-black cherries develop. Makes a fine hedge and windbreak. Used in Europe for topiary work.

19. CHERRY, WEEPING
(*Prunus serrulata 'Kiku-shidare-zakura'*)

Height: 8 ft.
Deciduous
Season of Flowering: Spring
Fruit
Fragrant
Location: full sun
Soil: average
Propagation: softwood cuttings
Budding and grafting

Zone 6

A weeping form. Profusion of fragrant, airy, fairy double pink flowers spill and trail from bush. Prefers a little winter, not for deep South. Hardy to zero.

20. CHERRY, YOSHINO
(*Prunus yedoensis 'Akebono'*)

Height: to 25 ft.
Deciduous
Season of Flowering: Spring
Fruit
Fragrant
Location: full sun
Soil: average
Propagation: softwood cuttings
Budding and grafting

Zone 6

Branches hidden by clouds of sweet-scented shell pink bloom. Same species as the famous Japanese Cherry Trees in Washington, D. C. Oriental symbol of wealth and prosperity.

21. CHOKEBERRY, RED
(*Aronia arbutifolia*)

Height: 8–12 ft.
Deciduous
Season of Flowering: Spring
Fruit
Colorful fall foliage
Location: full sun
Soil: adaptable
Propagation: seeds, division of clumps, softwood
    cuttings

Zone 5

Flowers like small white apple blossoms open in clusters. Decorative fruit resembling tiny red apples hangs on all winter. Leaves red in the fall. Dense foliage is an invitation to small birds to nest.

22. CORNELIAN CHERRY
(*Cornus mas*)

Height: 15–20 ft.
Deciduous
Season of Flowering: Spring
Fruit
Colorful foliage in fall
Location: full sun, light shade
Soil: average
Propagation: seeds, softwood cuttings
Zone 4

Tight clusters of bright yellow flowers along the branches create a haze of gold. The edible scarlet plum-like fruits are beloved by birds. Brilliant autumn foliage. Thrives to 20° below zero. One of the first shrubs to bloom in spring in the north.

23. COTONEASTER, ROCK
(*Cotoneaster horizontalis*)

Height: 3 ft.
Deciduous in North, Evergreen in South
Season of Flowering: Spring
Fruit
Location: full sun
Soil: rich loam, average
Propagation: softwood cuttings and seeds
Zones 4, 5, 6

Abundant white or pink flowers followed by decorative bright red berries. Attractive rugged little plant spreads horizontally to 6 ft. Splendid covering for steep banks.

24. CRABAPPLE, BECHTEL
(*Malus yedoensis plena bechtel*)

Height: 1–12 ft.
Deciduous
Season of flowering: Spring (alternate flowering)
Fruit, few
Spicy fragrance
Location: full sun
Soil: average
Propagation: budding or grafting
Zone 4

The spring flowers in their profusion all but conceal the branches. Each fragrant blossom is like a little rose, full and double when open. Buds are round as a ball. From first early bud to fully open blossoms, the tree presents a show unequalled for weeks. Highly decorative.

25. CRABAPPLE, KAIDO
(*Malus micromalus*)

Height: to 15 ft.
Deciduous
Season of Flowering: Spring
Fruit
Fragrant
Location: full sun
Soil: rich loam
Propagation: budding or grafting
Zone 5

Eventually a spread of 12 feet. Japanese origin. A blur of fragrant pink flowers hides the branches. Small, attractive, reddish fruits in fall. Tree has vase-like form.

26. CRABAPPLE, SARGENT
(*Malus sargentii*)

Height: to 8 ft.
Deciduous
Season of Flowering: Spring (alternate flowering)
Fruit
Colorful autumn foilage
Fragrant
Location: full sun
Soil: average
Propagation: seeds

Zone 4

A spicy fragrance from the single white flowers haunts the garden for weeks. Birds relish the dark red fruit.

27. CRABAPPLE, SHOWY
(*Malus floribunda*)

Height: 20–30 ft.
Deciduous
Season of Flowering: Spring
Colorful fruit
Fragrant
Location: full sun
Soil: average
Propagation: seeds
Zone 4

Graceful tree with curving branches. Covered with drifts of deeply scented pink flowers in spring. Small red to yellow crabapples in fall.

28. CURRANT, FLOWERING
(*Ribes sanguineum*)

Height: 5 ft.
Deciduous
Season of Flowering: Spring
Fruit: bluish black berries (sexes separate)
Location: full sun, light shade
Soil: average
Propagation: seeds and softwood cuttings
Zone 6

Deep crimson flowers in trailing racemes along stems. Thin plants after flowering, trimming a few stems back to ground level. Combine with forsythia and spring flowering bulbs.

29. DAPHNE
(*Daphne burkwoodii 'Somerset'*)

Height: 5 ft.
Deciduous in North, Evergreen in South
Season of Flowering: Spring
Location: full sun
Soil: alkaline
Propagation: difficult, seeds
Zone 5

Hardy. The fresh, cool fragrance of these light pink flowers mingles with other scents of spring. Appealing rich, dark green leaves. Desirable shrub.

30. DEUTZIA, SLENDER
(*Deutzia gracilis*)

Height: 1–4 ft.
Deciduous
Season of Flowering: Spring
Location: full sun, light shade
Soil: average
Propagation: softwood cuttings, division of roots
Zone 5

Good for hedges, foundation plantings. White flowers in terminal racemes decorative in arrangements. Prune off to the base ¼ of the old stems in early spring to retain vigorous growth. Tends to overgrow and when leggy is often broken in winter storms. Plant divides readily.

31. DOGWOOD
(*Cornus florida*)

Height: to 25 ft.
Deciduous
Season of Flowering: Spring
Scarlet fruit, scarlet leaves in fall
Location: full sun, light shade
Soil: acid, rich loam
Propagation: seeds, softwood cuttings, budding
and grafting
Zone 5

Like drifts of snow in a woodsy setting. Old time legend: wood from this tree was used for the Crucifixion. Note "cross arrangement" of bracts surrounding the flower, and the brown spots at the ends, a symbol of shame. Small tight buds of next year's flowers visible in the autumn when leaves fall.

32. DOGWOOD, PINK
(*Cornus florida rubra*)

Height: to 25 ft.
Deciduous
Season of Flowering: Spring
Fruit bright red in fall
Foliage also dazzling red in autumn
Location: full sun, light shade
Soil: acid, rich loam
Propagation: softwood cuttings, budding and
grafting

Zones 5, 6, 7

Clouds of appealing, strawberry ice cream pink bracts. Transplant with a ball of soil. Tonic made from the bark of certain dogwood varieties for fevers and that old time Victorian ailment called "the vapours".

33. ENKIANTHUS
(*Enkianthus campanulatus*)

Height: 6–12 ft.
Deciduous
Season of Flowering: Spring
Colorful
Location: full sun, light shade
Soil: acid
Propagation: softwood cuttings, seeds
Zone 5

Light yellow to orange flowers striped reddish-brown swing like little bells. Fine-toothed leaves, slightly waxy foliage turns brilliant red-orange in the fall. Soak in time of drought.

34. FIRETHORN
(*Pyracantha coccinea*)

Height: to 12 ft.
Evergreen
Season of Flowering: Spring
Fruit very decorative
Location: full sun, light shade
Soil: average
Propagation: softwood cuttings, seeds
Zones 5, 6

Thorns and spines along branches, leaves dark and glossy. Bunches of small white flowers, but grown mainly for the orange to scarlet fruit that lasts nearly all winter. Prune tops or from base to keep shapely. Can be trained as an espalier with proper pruning and wiring.

35. FORSYTHIA
(*Forsythia intermedia 'spectabilis'*)

Height: to 9 ft.
Deciduous
Season of Flowering: early Spring
Location: full sun, light shade
Soil: acid, adaptable
Propagation: softwood cuttings
Zone 5

Enchanting clouds of deep, yellow blossoms herald springtime. After flowering, prune old stalks to open center for air and sun. Allow branches to retain arching fountain effect. In January bring branches in, put in vase of water, and they will flower in ten days.

36. FOTHERGILLA
(*Fothergilla gardenii*)

Height: to 4 ft.
Deciduous
Season of Flowering: Spring
Colorful foliage in fall
Fragrant
Location: full sun
Soil: acid
Propagation: softwood cuttings, seeds
Zone 6

A dense bush. White stamened snowy flowers like small fluffy brushes. Grow in bright sun for spectacular orange-scarlet autumn leaves. Prune only to keep shapely.

37. GARDENIA
(*Gardenia jasminoides*)

Height: to 6 ft.
Evergreen
Season of Flowering: Spring, Summer, Fall
Fragrant
Location: full sun, light shade
Soil: acid, rich loam
Propagation: softwood cuttings
Zone 8

Waxy, white flowers with rich, haunting scent. Handsome glossy green leaves. Feed cottonseed meal. In the old time language of flowers, a blossom sent to a lady meant "I love you in secret."

38. GOLDEN CHAIN TREE
(*Laburnum watereri*)

Height: 15–20 ft.
Deciduous
Season of Flowering: Spring
Location: light shade
Soil: rich loam
Propagation: softwood cuttings, seed
Zone 5

Light green bark, gray-green leaves. Festooned with trailing racemes of golden wisteria-like flowers. In the old time language of flowers: "You have broken my heart." May be established with a single trunk by removing basal branches, or allowed to develop multiple stems.

39. HARDY-ORANGE
(*Poncirus trifoliata*)

Height: to 10 ft.
Deciduous
Season of Flowering: Spring
Fruit colorful
Fragrant
Location: full sun
Soil: rich loam
Propagation: seeds
Zone 6 (5 if protected)

Impenetrable hedge. Thorny green branches attractive in winter. Exotic perfume from spring flowers. Fruit inedible but appealing and fragrant.

40. HAWTHORN, ENGLISH 'PAUL'S SCARLET'
(*Crataegus oxyacantha*)

Height: to 15 ft.
Deciduous
Season of Flowering: Spring
Fruit
Location: full sun
Soil: average
Propagation: budding or grafting
Zone 4

Gay, double red flowers and bright scarlet fruit. Washington brought this bush to Mt. Vernon in 1792. Associated with May Day Frolics of Chaucer's time.

41. HAWTHORN; WASHINGTON THORN
(*Crataegus phaenopyrum*)

Height: to 20 ft.
Deciduous
Season of Flowering: Spring
Fruit
Location: full sun
Soil: average
Propagation: seeds
Zone 4

The stout, thorny branches grow horizontally. Clusters of appealing white spring flowers open in the spring. Glossy red fall fruits hang on for weeks. Used as pasture fences in Virginia.

42. HAZEL, AMERICAN
(*Corylus americana*)

Height: to 10 ft.
Deciduous
Season of Flowering: early Spring
Fruit
Location: full sun, no sun
Soil: rich loam
Propagation: softwood cuttings, seeds
Zones 4–9

Branches swing decorative brown and gold catkins in early spring. Grows wild from New England to Florida. You must compete with squirrels for the delicious nuts. Hardy, easy. Prefers moist coolness.

43. HOLLY-OLIVE
(*Osmanthus delavayi*)

Height: 6 ft.
Evergreen
Season of Flowering: Spring
Fruit
Fragrant
Location: full sun, light shade
Soil: rich loam
Propagation: softwood cuttings
Zone 8

Small creamy flowers deliciously fragrant with a fruity scent. Leaves resemble holly including the spine. Dark blue fruit. Choice for West Coast and Southern areas.

44. HONEYSUCKLE, TATARIAN
(*Lonicera tatarica*)

Height: to 10 ft.
Deciduous
Season of Flowering: Spring
Fruit
Location: full sun
Soil: average
Propagation: softwood cuttings
Zone 3

Native to Turkestan and Russia. A choice dense and spreading shrub from old European gardens. Cheery pink spring flowers. Sparkling red summer fruit. Lest it grow too large, cut to ground periodically, and never hesitate to remove unwanted branches.

45. JETBEAD
(*Rhodotypos scandens*)

Height: to 6 ft.
Deciduous
Season of Flowering: Spring, Summer
Fruit
Location: full sun, light shade
Soil: average
Propagation: softwood cuttings, seed
Zone 5

White, four-petalled flowers surprise you in summer too. Showy black fruits. Open, airy bush. Cut to ground each spring for compact growth.

46. JEWEL BERRY
(*Callicarpa dichotoma*)

Height: to 5 ft.
Deciduous
Season of Flowering: late Spring, Summer, Fall
Fruit
Location: full sun, light shade
Soil: rich loam
Propagation: softwood cuttings, seed
Zone 5

Native to China. Small pink flowers followed by violet berries, which last weeks in winter. Excellent trimmed off and used in arrangements. Prune drastically in late winter.

47. KERRIA
(*Kerria japonica*)

Height: to 6 ft.
Deciduous
Season of Flowering: Spring
Color in fall
Location: full sun, light shade
Soil: average
Propagation: softwood cuttings, seed; also
   divide roots
Zones 6, 7

Affectionately called 'Dandelion bush' because of vivid, gold flowers that star green branches in spring. Stalks remain bright green all winter and are colorful in the snow. Divide roots in March, share with friends.

48. LEUCOTHOË
(*Leucothoë fontanesiana*)

Height: 4 ft.
Evergreen
Season of Flowering: Spring
Colorful
Fragrant
Location: light shade
Soil: acid, rich loan
Propagation: hardwood cuttings
Zones 6, 7

Broad-leaved evergreen of graceful, arching habit. Leaves bronze-red through winter. Flowers, waxy-white and bell-shaped, strung along the branches beneath foliage. Grows wild in Southern mountains. Remains green and attractive indoors in water for weeks.

49. LILAC, CHINESE
(*Syringa* x *chinensis*)

Height: 12–15 ft.
Deciduous
Season of Flowering: Spring
Fragrant
Location: full sun
Soil: average
Propagation: softwood cuttings
Zone 5

A graceful open shrub with purple and white blooms in loosely put together clusters. May need lime annually. To make a lilac hedge plant three feet apart. To be able to reach and enjoy flowers from the ground, prune immediately after blooming. Remove ¼ to ⅕ of the older stems close to the ground.

50. LILAC, COMMON
(*Syringa vulgaris*)

Height: to 15 ft.
Deciduous
Season of Flowering: Spring
Fragrant
Location: full sun
Soil: average
Propagation: softwood cuttings
Zone 3

Deeply fragrant, wonderful cut flowers. Plant near window and scent drifts in. White and lavender. In old time England people cleaned pith out of the stalks and used them for pipe stems. Prune out ¼ to ⅕ of older stems after blooming to keep bush within bounds and shapely. Cut at ground level. Set out with graft below ground level. Remove all shoots below graft.

51. LILAC, PERSIAN
(*Syringa* x *persica*)

Height: to 6 ft.
Deciduous
Season of Flowering: Spring
Fragrant
Location: full sun
Soil: average
Propagation: softwood cuttings
Zone 5

Pale lavender and white, sweet spicy-scented flowers. Excellent screen planting. Remove suckers at plant base annually. The bush is host to catbirds and sparrows who build in branches.

52. MAGNOLIA, SAUCER
(*Magnolia* x *soulangeana*)

Height: to 25 ft.
Deciduous
Season of Flowering: Spring
Fragrant
Location: full sun
Soil: rich loam
Propagation: softwood cuttings, seed
Zone 5

Pleasing, smooth gray bark. Showy white flowers with purple petals outside. Bush moves best when in active vigorous spring growth. Adjusts rapidly to new surroundings. Shelter from wind.

53. MAGNOLIA, STAR
(*Magnolia stellata*)

Height: to 15 ft.
Decidous
Season of Flowering: early Spring
Fragrant
Location: full sun, light shade
Soil: rich loam
Propagation: softwood cuttings, seed
Zone 5

Pure white petals like shiny satin ribbon compose the flower. Interesting furry buds decorate the tree weeks ahead. Don't crowd other shrubs near. Blooms at 2 feet. Observe how the vivid-colored seeds slowly descend on threads and then are grabbed by birds.

54. MAHONIA, LEATHERLEAF
(*Mahonia bealei*)

Height: 8–12 ft.
Evergreen
Season of Flowering: Spring–early
Fragrant flowers
Fruit: highly decorative
Colorful leaves in fall
Location: light shade, no sun
Soil: rich loam
Propagation: hardwood cuttings

Zone 6

Fragrant flowers in large yellow clusters come in late winter, among the very first. Rugged handsome bush with yellow wood and finely toothed leaves. Blue-black berries hang in clusters, suggesting grapes. Rare, easy.

55. MAHONIA; OREGON HOLLY-GRAPE
(*Mahonia aquifolium*)

Height: to 5 ft.
Evergreen
Season of Flowering: Spring
Fruit
Colorful fall foliage
Fragrant
Location: light shade, no sun
Soil: rich loam
Propagation: hardwood cuttings

Zone 5

Clusters of small yellow flowers bright at branch tips in late winter. Bunches of deep blue berries follow blooms. Leathery foliage with spines like holly turns shiny bronze in fall and winter.

56. MEXICAN-ORANGE
(*Choisya ternata*)

Height: to 6 ft.
Deciduous or Evergreen: Evergreen
Season of Flowering: Spring
Fruit
Fragrant
Location: full sun
Soil: rich loam
Propagation: seeds
Zone 8

Clusters of fragrant, white starry flowers terminate the shoots in early spring and occasionally through the summer. Neat, compact bush with aromatic leaves. Is decorative when used to define entrances.

57. MOCK ORANGE
(*Philadelphus x lemoinei*)

Height: 4–8 ft.
Deciduous
Season of Flowering: Spring
Fragrant
Location: full sun, light shade
Soil: rich loam
Propagation: softwood and hardwood cuttings
Zone 5

Each white, 2-inch flower extremely fragrant. Water in drought. Prune drastically after flowering. Cut out old tough stems at ground level every few years.

58. MOCK ORANGE, SWEET
(*Philadelphus coronarius*)

Height: to 10 ft.
Deciduous
Season of Flowering: Spring
Fragrant
Location: full sun, light shade
Soil: rich loam
Propagation: softwood cuttings
Zone 4

Upright branching shrub with single white, orange-blossom scented flowers. Prune after flowering; open center to encourage new growth which will be graceful and arching.

59. MOUNTAIN-ASH, AMERICAN
(*Sorbus americana*)

Height: to 20 ft.
Deciduous
Season of Flowering: Spring
Fruit
Location: full sun, light shade
Soil: rich loam
Propagation: seeds, budding and grafting
Zone 4

Smooth gray bark. White flowers in flat clusters. Brilliant coral red berries, fall and into winter. An old Nordic belief: protects you from magic and sorcery.

60. MULBERRY, WHITE
(*Morus alba*)

Height: to 25 ft.
Deciduous
Season of Flowering: Spring
Fruit
Location: full sun
Soil: average
Propagation: softwood cuttings, seeds
Zone 4

A tree that brings you flowers, fruits, birds a-plenty. Especially loved by cardinals. White berries delectable. Soft early spring catkins. Old time symbol of wisdom. Bake a mulberry pie.

61. OLEANDER
(*Nerium oleander*)

Height: to 20 ft.
Evergreen
Season of Flowering: Spring
Fragrant
Location: full sun
Soil: average
Propagation: softwood cuttings
Zone 8

Double, single flowers at branch tips. Pink, white, red, rose. Narrow gray-green leaves. Thrives in dry areas. Cuttings readily root in water for new plants. Old time symbol of beauty and grace.

62. ORCHID TREE, PURPLE
(*Bauhinia variegata*)

Height: to 20 ft.
Deciduous
Season of Flowering: Spring
Location: full sun
Soil: average
Propagation: softwood cuttings, seeds
Zone 9

From India and China. A charming, slow-growing tree for the deep South. Covered in spring with large flowers, deep pinkish-lavender, touched purple. Note interesting gold-tipped stamens.

63. PARROTIA
(*Parrotia persica*)

Height: to 15 ft.
Deciduous
Season of Flowering: Spring
Colorful in fall
Location: full sun, light shade
Soil: average
Propagation: softwood cuttings
Zone 5

Furry brown flowers, white inside with long arching stamens. Red or gold fall foliage. Bark peels off in places leaving white beneath and creates interesting winter patterns somewhat like the sycamore.

64. PAULOWNIA, IMPERIALIS
(*Paulownia tomentosa*)

Height: to 30 ft.
Deciduous
Season of Flowering: Spring
Location: full sun
Soil: average
Propagation: seeds, root cuttings
Zone 6

Violet tubular flowers rise like an upright wisteria raceme. Large dark brown seed pods follow. Grows wild from New Jersey southward. Shelter from wind.

65. PEACH, DOUBLE RED FLOWERING
(*Prunus persica 'Rubroplena'*)

Height: to 20 ft.
Deciduous
Season of Flowering: Spring
Fruit
Fragrant
Location: full sun
Soil: average
Propagation: budding or grafting
Zone 5

A spring garden feature. Large double red flowers crowd every twig. Prune severely after bloom. Next season's blossoms grow on this year's new wood.

66. PEACH, FLOWERING
(*Prunus Persica*)

Height: to 20 ft.
Deciduous
Season of Flowering: Spring
Fruit
Fragrant
Location: full sun
Soil: average
Propagation: softwood cuttings, budding and grafting

Zone 5

Blossoms red, pink, white. For Southern gardens. In rural China the stones are made into good luck charms for the children to wear.

67. PEARL-BUSH
(*Exochorda giraldii, var. Wilsonii*)

Height: to 15 ft.
Deciduous
Season of Flowering: Spring
Location: full sun
Soil: rich loam
Propagation: softwood cuttings, seeds
Zone 5

Native to China. Buds like clusters of white beads, opening to flowers with distinctive green calyx. Plant with peat. Prune after bloom for an abundance of flowers next year.

68. PEARL-BUSH
(*Exochorda racemosa*)

Height: to 9 ft.
Deciduous
Season of Flowering: Spring
Location: full sun
Propagation: softwood cuttings, seeds
Soil: rich loam
Zone 4

Native to the Orient. Five-petalled crinkle-edged white flowers. Most attractive and easy to raise. Plant with plenty of peat and organic matter.

69. PEONY, TREE
(*Paeonia lutea*)

Height: to 3 ft.
Deciduous
Season of Flowering: Spring
Fragrant
Location: full sun
Soil: rich loam
Propagation: seeds, division in Fall
Zone 5

Gold flowers trail over plant. Foliage makes cool green summer bouquet. Lasts indoors for weeks. It is the Japanese symbol of prosperity. Discovered in China, 1900.

70. PEONY, TREE
(*Paeonia suffruticosa*)

Height: to 6 ft.
Deciduous
Season of Flowering: Spring
Fragrant
Location: full sun, light shade
Soil: rich loam
Propagation: seeds, division in Fall
Zone 5

Huge frilled and crinkled flowers, pink, white, or red with yellow centers. Protect from winter winds. For prolific bloom, feed leaf mold, well-rotted manure, wood ashes, superphosphates.

71. PHOTINIA
(*Photinia serrulata*)

Height: to 12 ft.
Deciduous
Season of Flowering: Spring
Fruit
Colorful in autumn
Location: full sun
Soil: rich loam
Propagation: softwood cuttings, seeds
Zone 7

From China. Tiny white flowers in flat clusters. Yellow leaves in fall. Brilliant scarlet fruits draw the birds. May be an espalier. Shiny leaves bronze when new. Give ample room.

72. PITTOSPORUM
(*Pittosporum tobira*)

Height: to 10 ft.
Deciduous
Season of Flowering: Spring
Fragrant
Location: full sun, light shade
Soil: rich loam
Propagation: softwood cuttings
Zone 8

Thrives at the seashore. Large, spreading shrub, leathery deep green leaves, creamy white flowers. Orange-blossom scent. Highly decorative garden feature.

73. PLUM, FLOWERING
(*Prunus blireana*)

Height: to 15 ft.
Deciduous
Season of Flowering: Spring
Fruit
Fragrant
Location: full sun
Soil: average
Propagation: budding or grafting
Zone 5

Branches festooned with gay double Valentine-pink flowers just before the red-bronze leaves appear. Foliage deepens in full sun. In language of flowers: "Keep your promises."

74. PLUM, FLOWERING
(*Prunus cerasifera* 'Thundercloud')

Height: to 20 ft.
Deciduous
Season of Flowering: Spring
Colorful Foliage
Fruit
Fragrant
Location: full sun
Soil: average
Propagation: budding or grafting

Zone 3

Gracefully rounded well-shaped tree with leaves rich red. Quantities of pink flowers in spring. Slow growing. Bring branches indoors for forcing.

75. PLUM, FLOWERING
(*Prunus triloba*)

Height: to 15 ft.
Deciduous
Season of Flowering: Spring
Fruit
Fragrant
Location: full sun
Soil: average
Propagation: softwood cuttings; seed
Zone 5

Bright, pink, double flowers hide all stems. Attractive with spring bulbs beneath. Prune only to shape. May be espaliered against wall or fence.

76. PLUM, PURPLE-LEAF
(*Prunus cerasifera* 'Pissardi')

Height: to 20 ft.
Deciduous
Season of Flowering: Spring
Fruit
Fragrant
Location: full sun
Soil: average; adaptable
Propagation: budding, grafting
Zone 3

Grows erect in fan-like form. 15 ft. spread. Distinctive purple-red foliage. Small single flowers emerge from dark, red leaf buds. Adapts to almost any soil.

77. PUSSY WILLOW, FRENCH
(*Salix caprea*)

Height: to 10 ft.
Deciduous
Season of Flowering: Spring
Location: full sun, light shade
Soil: average
Propagation: softwood cuttings
Zone 4

Native to Asia and Europe. Catkins much larger and slightly brushed with pink. Pick for indoor enjoyment in winter. Leave branches in water until they root, and each one becomes a new shrub.

78. QUINCE, FLOWERING
(*Chaenomeles speciosa*)

Height: to 6 ft.
Deciduous
Season of Flowering: Spring
Fruit
Location: light shade
Soil: acid
Propagation: softwood cuttings
Zone 4

Red to white to orange flowers greet the spring in great abundance. At summer's end apple-shaped fruits ripen whose spicy scent fills the whole garden. Makes delectable jelly. Spreading habit of growth. Thrives against walls and fences where it may attain a height of 10–15 ft.

79. QUINCE, JAPANESE
(*Chaenomeles speciosa lagenaria*)

Height: 6–10 ft.
Deciduous
Season of Flowering: Spring
Fruit
Location: full sun, light shade
Soil: adaptable
Propagation: softwood cuttings
Zone 5

Scarlet, white, pink, orange flowers appear in abundance, in the heart of a thorny bush. Fruit yellow-green, 2 inches in diameter. Thrives against a wall or fence.

80. REDBUD, EASTERN; JUDAS TREE
(*Cercis canadensis*)

Height: to 25 ft.
Deciduous
Season of Flowering: Spring
Location: full sun, light shade
Soil: average
Propagation: seeds
Zone 4

Graceful slender tree. Enchanting pink-lavender flowers decorate branches. Thrives on roadsides, along borders of streams. Grows abundantly on upper Potomac, in Ozarks, north to New Haven, Connecticut.

81. RHODODENDRON, CAROLINA
(*Rhododendron carolinianum*)

Height: to 15 ft.
Evergreen
Season of Flowering: Spring
Location: light shade, no sun
Soil: acid, rich loam
Propagation: hardwood cuttings
Zone 5

Flowers rosy-purple, pink, white. Member of broad and illustrious family that grows wild in the South, especially all through the Blue Ridge mountains. Cultivated in northern gardens. Thrives in woodlands, along stream banks. Mulch with decomposing leaves. Water in drought.

82. RHODODENDRON
(*Rhododendron fortunei*)

Height: to 10 ft.
Evergreen
Season of Flowering: Spring
Location: light shade
Soil: acid, rich loam
Propagation: hardwood cuttings
Zone 6

Broad leaved. Flowers white to pale pink. Leathery thick foliage curls tight into cigar shape in winter cold. Uncurls as temperature rises.

83. RHODODENDRON, CATAWBA
(*Rhododendron catawbiense*)

Height: to 8 ft.
Evergreen
Season of Flowering: Spring, Summer
Location: light shade, no sun
Soil: acid, rich loam
Propagation: hardwood cuttings
Zone 4

Wild in mountains of Virginia and North Carolina where it covers whole mountainsides. Peaty acid soil. Compact shrub, lustrous green leaves, white, pink, purple flowers. Among most beautiful of native plants.

84. ST. JOHNSWORT
(*Hypericum calycinum*)

Height: to 1½ ft.
Deciduous
Season of Flowering: Spring, Summer
Location: full sun, light shade
Soil: adaptable
Propagation: softwood cuttings, seed
Zone 6

Golden 3-inch blooms with quantities of stamens. An old European rural custom on St. John's Eve in June people walked through the smoke of fires of St. Johnswort wood to increase their courage and strength.

85. SAPPHIREBERRY, ASIATIC SWEETLEAF
(*Symplocos paniculata*)

Height: to 35 ft.
Deciduous
Season of Flowering: Spring
Fruit
Fragrant
Location: full sun, light shade
Soil: average
Propagation: seeds
Zone 5

Native to Japan and China. Grows like a small tree. Sweet-scented white flowers. Attractive blue berries appreciated in fall by garden lovers and birds alike. Hardy, easy.

86. SHADBLOW
(*Amelanchier x grandiflora*)

Height: to 25 ft.
Deciduous
Season of Flowering: Spring
Fruit
Location: full sun
Soil: average
Propagation: seeds
Zone 4

Blooms when shad rush up streams to spawn, hence name. Five-petalled flowers at twig tips decorate branches in April. Edible fruits follow much relished by the birds. Trim stalks in late winter for indoor flowers. Bark is mottled gray. Keep dead and broken branches pruned off.

87. SHRUBBY CINQUEFOIL
(*Potentilla fruticosa* 'Gold Drop')

Height: to 3 ft.
Deciduous
Season of Flowering: Spring, Summer
Location: full sun
Soil: average
Propagation: softwood cuttings
Zone 2

Compact little bush covered with flowers of gold that keep opening off and on all summer. Tough and hardy. Thrives to 40° below zero.

88. SILVERBELL TREE
(*Halesia carolina*)

Height: to 30 ft.
Deciduous
Season of Flowering: Spring
Colorful in fall
Location: full sun, light shade
Soil: rich loam
Propagation: softwood cuttings
Zone 5

In mid-May every branch and twig swings small snowy bells. Later four-winged fruits drift to ground. Clear yellow leaves in autumn.

89. SKIMMIA
(*Skimmia japonica*)

Height: to 4 ft.
Evergreen
Season of Flowering: Spring
Fruit in fall
Fragrant
Location: light shade
Soil: acid, rich loam
Propagation: softwood cuttings; seed
Zone 6

Native to Japan. Small, fragrant, creamy flowers at branch tips. Brilliant, scarlet berries in fall. For fruit have two plants, male and female. Leathery, lustrous, light green leaves. Plant with plenty of compost.

90. SNOW-WREATH
(*Neviusia alabamensis*)

Height: to 5 ft.
Deciduous
Season of Flowering: Spring
Location: full sun, light shade
Soil: average
Propagation: softwood cuttings, plant suckers
Zone 5

A cloud of white from a distance. Feathery flowers, mostly stamens, cover rounded shrub. Rare. For new bushes replant suckers found at base.

91. SPICE BUSH
(*Lindera benzoin*)

Height: to 12 ft.
Deciduous
Season of Flowering: Spring
Fruit
Colorful foliage
Location: full sun, light shade
Soil: average
Propagation: seeds
Zone 4

Quaint, fringed golden blossoms unfold at twig joints to welcome spring. Red berries come later. Thrives along streams in semi-shade with moisture nearby. Easy. Autumn foliage gold.

92. SPIRAEA, DOUBLE; BRIDALWREATH
(*Spiraea prunifolia*)

Height: to 8 ft.
Deciduous
Season of Flowering: Spring
Colorful fall foliage
Fragrant
Location: full sun, light shade
Soil: average
Propagation: softwood cuttings
Zone 5

From Eastern Asia. Tiny double flowers smother the bush for about three weeks. Narrow leaves orange in autumn. Used in old-fashioned wedding bouquets. Brought good luck, health, prosperity to young couple.

93. SPIRAEA, GARLAND
(*Spiraea x arguta*)

Height: to 6 ft.
Deciduous
Season of Flowering: Spring
Fragrant
Location: full sun, light shade
Soil: average
Propagation: softwood cuttings
Zone 4

A fine foliaged shrub with clusters of small white flowers along arching branches in fountain-like effect. Transplants easily spring or fall.

94. SPIRAEA, THUNBERG'S
(*Spiraea thunbergii*)

Height: to 4 ft.
Deciduous
Season of Flowering: Spring
Colorful in autumn
Fragrant
Location: full sun, light shade
Soil: average
Propagation: softwood cuttings
Zone 4

Flowers before leaves. Upright slender branches laden with umbels of snowy florets. Bush may be cut entirely back near base and new shoots emerge. Do this periodically to keep bush shapely. Makes an excellent hedge. Narrow foliage yellow in autumn. Very hardy: will stand 15° below zero. Give well-drained soil.

95. STRAWBERRY-SHRUB; SWEET SHRUB
(*Calycanthus floridus*)

Height: to 7 ft.
Deciduous
Season of Flowering: Spring, Summer
Fragrant
Location: light shade
Soil: rich loam
Propagation: seed
Zone 4

Attractive foliage dark and glossy. Many-petalled reddish-brown flowers, when crushed, smell of ripe pineapple. Children tied it in handkerchiefs to cheer their spirits through old-fashioned long sermons and hard church benches.

96. TAMARISK
(*Tamarix parviflora*)

Height: to 15 ft.
Deciduous
Season of Flowering: Spring
Location: full sun
Soil: acid, rich loam, adaptable
Propagation: softwood or hardwood cuttings
Zone 4

A veil of silvery blue-green foliage covered by airy rose-pink flowers. Blossoms and foliage both are lovely to cut for indoor bouquets. Thrives at seashore and in deserty Southwest. Leaves are needle-like and fringe reddish branches.

97. VIBURNUM
(*Viburnum wrightii*)

Height: to 6 ft.
Deciduous
Season of Flowering: Spring
Fruit
Colorful autumn foliage
Location: full sun, light shade
Soil: rich loam
Propagation: softwood cuttings
Zone 5

Deeply veined metallic green leaves. White spring flowers. Glistening red fruits. In fall foliage turns rich crimson. Sturdy and trouble free.

98. VIBURNUM, BURKWOOD'S
(*Viburnum x burkwoodii*)

Height: to 6 ft.
Deciduous
Season of Flowering: Spring
Fragrant
Location: light shade, no sun
Soil: rich loam
Propagation: softwood cuttings
Zone 5

Clusters of white flowers flushed pink with deep gardenia-like scent. Give good loam, moist, well-drained semi-shady spot. Hardy in city back yards.

99. VIBURNUM, DOUBLEFILE
(*Viburnum tomentosum*)

Height: to 9 ft.
Deciduous
Season of Flowering: Spring
Fruit
Colorful autumn leaves
Location: full sun, light shade
Soil: rich loam
Propagation: softwood cuttings
Zone 4

Flat clusters of showy white flowers fade to pink. Red berries in summer, leaves bronzy red in fall. Give well-drained, moist, rich soil. Feed peat, compost, well rotted manure.

100. VIBURNUM, FRAGRANT
(*Viburnum carlesii*)

Height: to 6 ft.
Deciduous
Season of Flowering: Spring
Fragrant
Location: full sun, light shade
Soil: rich loam
Propagation: softwood cuttings
Zone 4

Showy heads of white flowers tinged with apple blossom pink. Dry on sunny window sill for fragrant sachets in linen closet. Feed well-rotted manure and put several shovelfuls in hole when planting.

101. WEIGELA
(*Weigela florida*)

Height: to 7 ft.
Deciduous
Season of Flowering: Spring, Summer
Location: full sun
Soil: rich loam
Propagation: softwood cuttings
Zone 5

Prefers rich, moist soil and freedom from encroaching roots. Pink flowers nearly hide the graceful arching foliage. Hardy to zero degrees F.

102. WINTER-HAZEL, CHINESE
(*Corylopsis sinensis*)

Height: 8–12 ft.
Deciduous
Season of Flowering: Spring
Fragrant
Location: full sun, light shade
Soil: rich loam
Propagation: softwood cuttings, seeds
Zone 5

Countless trailing racemes of fragrant yellow flowers followed by gray-green toothed leaves. Give well-drained humusy soil and protect from winter wind. Fine in Southwest.

103. WINTERSWEET
(*Chimonanthus praecox*)

Height: to 9 ft.
Deciduous
Season of Flowering: early Spring
Fragrant
Location: light shade
Soil: light and sandy, rich loam
Propagation: softwood cuttings, layers, seeds
Zone 7

Pale yellow flowers with dark brown centers appear before the foliage. Blooms hauntingly sweet and fragrant. Compact shrub. Plant in protected location. Prefers winter sun and summer shade.

104. ZENOBIA, DUSTY
(*Zenobia pulverulenta*)

Height: to 4 ft.
Evergreen in South, deciduous in North
Season of Flowering: Spring
Location: light shade
Soil: acid
Propagation: softwood cuttings, seed
Zone 6

Member of family Ericaceae. Showy little bell-shaped white flowers in clusters of two dozen or more decorate bush. Plant with peat moss.

Summer Flowering

105. ABELIA, GLOSSY
(*Abelia grandiflora*)

Height: 4–6 ft.
Evergreen in the South, deciduous in the North
Season of Flowering: Summer, Fall
Colorful
Location: full sun
Soil: rich loam
Propagation: softwood cuttings
Zone 5

Sprays of small bell-shaped white flowers flushed pink grow at stem tips. Fine in bouquets. Open-branching bush, shiny green leaves bronze in the autumn. Protect from winds, cold winter, or drying in summer. Easy.

106. ACACIA, ROSE
(*Robinia hispida*)

Height: 3–7 ft.
Deciduous
Season of Flowering: Summer
Location: full sun, light shade
Soil: adaptable
Propagation: seeds and root cuttings
Zone 5

Flower stems and purple pods hairy as twigs. Ideal for naturalizing where rapid spreading plants are desired. Thrives in sandy seashore soil. Soft green fern-like foliage trails clusters of pink sweet pea-like flowers. Bristly stems are red in winter. Tends to spread by runners where not wanted. Pull these up back to parent plant to keep within bounds.

107. AZALEA, WHITE SWAMP
(*Rhododendron viscosum*)

Height: to 10 ft.
Deciduous
Season of Flowering: Summer
Fragrant
Location: light shade, no sun
Soil: acid, rich loam
Propagation: softwood cuttings, seed
Zone 3

An exciting flower to plant along stream banks or to naturalize in any moist shady area. Flaring funnel-shaped flowers pink or white with interesting stamens and a sweet scent. Attracts and plays host to bees, butterflies, and exotic night moths.

108. BEAUTY BUSH
(*Kolkwitzia amabilis*)

Height: to 12 ft.
Deciduous
Season of Flowering: Summer
Location: full sun, light shade
Soil: average
Propagation: softwood cuttings
Zone 4

Originally from China. Graceful arching bush. Branches covered with plumes of delicate pink-orange bell-like flowers. Hardy in heat, wind, and to 10° below zero. Give ample room. Easy.

109. BLUE-SPIRAEA
(*Caryopteris incana*)

Height: 3–6 ft.
Deciduous
Season of Flowering: Summer, Fall
Location: full sun
Soil: rich loam, light sandy
Propagation: softwood cuttings
Zone 5

From China. Soft violet-blue flowers lovely in arrangements. Valuable fall flowering shrub. Prune annually to keep compact. Dies to ground in northern winters. Easy.

110. BUCKEYE BOTTLEBRUSH
(*Aesculus parviflora*)

Height: 8–12 ft.
Deciduous
Season of Flowering: Summer
Location: full sun
Soil: rich loam
Propagation: seed, suckers.
Zone 4

Soft, furry, white flowers in appealing upright one-foot panicles. Give moist situation. Separate suckers in spring for new plants. According to old-time lore, this shrub brought good luck wherever it grew.

111. BUTTERFLY BUSH
(*Buddleia davidi*)

Height: 8 ft.
Deciduous
Season of Flowering: Summer, Fall
Fragrant
Location: full sun
Soil: rich loam
Propagation: softwood cuttings
Zone 5

Native to China. Ten-inch spires of sweet-scented tiny florets, white, pink, lavender, or purple. Called Summer Lilac. Prune severely each March. Propagates easily from cuttings.

112. CINQUEFOIL BUSH
(*Potentilla fruticosa veitchii*, 'Mount Everest')

Height: to 3 ft.
Deciduous
Season of Flowering: Summer, Fall
Location: full sun
Soil: adaptable
Propagation: softwood cuttings
Zone 2

Continuous clear yellow flowers from early summer to frost. Fern-like leaves. Makes fine hedge. Hardy through the roughest winters. Needs absolutely no care.

113. CRAPE MYRTLE
(*Lagerstroemia indica*)

Height: to 20 ft.
Deciduous
Season of Flowering: Summer
Location: full sun
Soil: rich loam
Propagation: softwood and hardwood cuttings
Zone 7

The bush is lilac-shaped with interesting golden tan bark. Every branch is tipped with tossing plumes of crinkly flowers in white, pink, red, or lavender. Blooms best inland. Makes a beautiful hedge to mark a boundary line.

114. DEUTZIA, LEMOINE
(*Deutzia x lemoinei*)

Height: to 7 ft.
Deciduous
Season of Flowering: Summer
Location: full sun, light shade
Soil: average
Propagation: softwood cuttings
Zone 4

White flowers in small panicles. Prune annually after blooms. Hardy, dependable. Water in drought. Oriental tinkers used foliage to polish brass.

115. DOGWOOD, JAPANESE
(*Cornus kousa*)

Height: to 20 ft.
Deciduous
Season of Flowering: Summer
Fruit
Colorful foliage
Location: full sun, light shade
Soil: acid, rich loam
Propagation: softwood cuttings, seed
Zone 5

Each bract gracefully pointed. Fruit resembles a strawberry. Leaves scarlet in fall. Give dogwoods ample humus, mulch with old leaves. Feed well-rotted manure annually.

116. FALSE-SPIRAEA, KASHMIR
(*Sorbaria aitchisonii*)

Height: 4–8 ft.
Deciduous
Season of Flowering: Summer
Location: full sun, light shade
Soil: rich loam
Propagation: softwood cuttings
Zone 6

Appealing white flower panicles carried on red stems. Attractive fern-like pale green foilage. Naturalize in front of evergreens. Grows fast in moist soil. Cut to ground each spring.

The following colored illustrations are numbered to correspond with the text. Spring flowering shrubs (1–104) are described on pages 11–45; summer flowering (105–160) on pages 49–67; fall flowering (161–163) on page 71, and winter flowering (164–169) on pages 75–76.

Spring Flowering

1   2   3   4

5   6   7   8

9

10

11

12

13

14

15

16

17

18

19

20

21   22   23   24

25   26   27   28

29   30   31   32

33

34

35

36

37

38

39

40

41

42

43

44

45

46

47

48

49

50

51

52

53

54

55

56

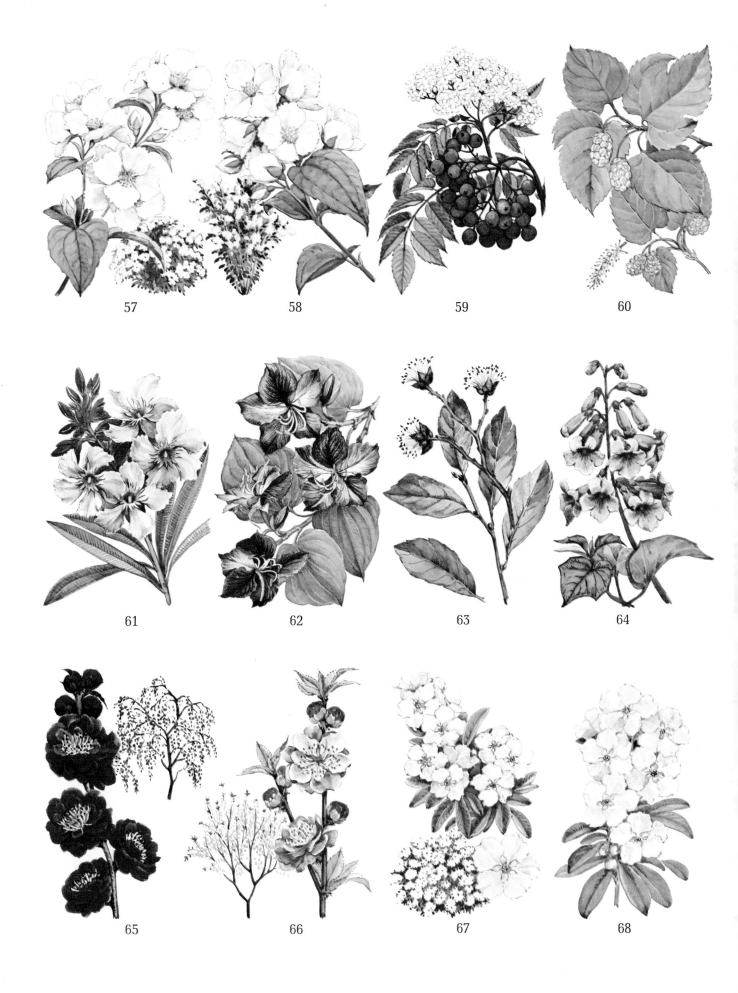

57

58

59

60

61

62

63

64

65

66

67

68

69   70   71   72

73   74   75   76

77   78   79   80

81

82

83

84

85

86

87

88

89

90

91

92

93

94

95

96

97

98

99

100

101

102

103

104

Summer Flowering

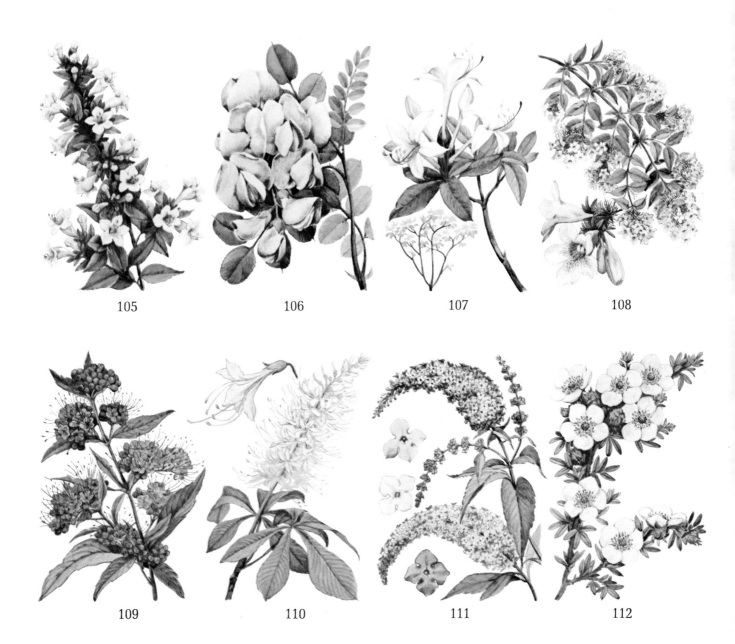

105   106   107   108

109   110   111   112

113

114

115

116

117

118

119

120

121

122

123

124

125

126

127

128

129

130

131

132

133

134

135

136

137

138

139

140

141

142

143

144

145

146

147

148

149

150

151

152

153

154

155

156

157

158

159

160

Fall & Winter Flowering

161

162

163

164

165

166

167

168

169

117. FRANKLIN TREE
(*Franklinia alatamaha*)

Height: to 30 ft.
Deciduous
Season of Flowering: Summer, Fall
Location: full sun
Soil: rich loam
Propagation: softwood cuttings
Zone 5

Named for Benjamin Franklin. Taller in mild climates. Yellow-centered, white flowers. Shiny leaves turn deep red in fall. Protect the first few winters with leaves.

118. FRINGETREE
(*Chionanthus virginicus*)

Height: to 30 ft.
Deciduous
Season of Flowering: Summer
Fruit
Fragrant
Location: full sun
Soil: adaptable
Propagation: seed
Zone 4

Annually tree is ornamented with a feathery fringe of deeply-scented white blossoms. Grow two, male and female. Female bears attractive blue fall fruits.

119. FUCHSIA
(*Fuchsia magellanica*)

Height: to 5 ft.
Deciduous
Season of Flowering: Summer
Location: light shade
Soil: acid, rich loam
Propagation: softwood cuttings
Zone 7

Fairy-like red and blue flowers, each like a small poised toe-dancer, swing in the breeze. Host to flocks of humming birds who visit daily seeking nectar. Thrives where heavy dew falls. You may remove lateral shoot development and keep pruned to a standard to form a tree fuchsia.

120. GENISTA
(*Genista cinerea*)

Height: to 3 ft.
Deciduous
Season of Flowering: Summer
Location: full sun
Soil: average, light sandy
Propagation: hardwood cuttings
Zone 7

Yellow flowers in trailing racemes. Flourishes in hot, dry sunny situations and in sandy soil. Do not disturb once it is set out.

121. GOLDEN RAIN TREE
(*Koelreuteria paniculata*)

Height: to 25 ft.
Deciduous
Season of Flowering: Summer
Location: full sun
Soil: adaptable
Propagation: seed
Zone 5

Attractive foilage decorated with erect panicles of bright yellow flowers. Blossoms rain to earth —hence the name—turning ground to a fresh gold carpet for days. Tolerates heat. Shelter from wind.

122. HARLEQUIN; GLORY-BOWER
(*Clerodendrum trichotomum*)

Height: to 9 ft.
Deciduous
Season of Flowering: Summer, Fall
Fruit
Fragrant
Location: full sun
Soil: rich loam
Propagation: softwood cuttings
Zone 6

Small clusters of fragrant white flowers in August. Bright blue berries create a showy fall display. Interesting leaves, gray and hairy.

123. HEATH, BELL
(*Erica cinerea*)

Height: to 2 ft.
Evergreen
Season of Flowering: Summer
Colorful
Location: full sun, light shade
Soil: light sandy
Propagation: soft and hardwood cuttings
Zone 5

A rounded shrub strung with delicate flowers, white to purple. Dry for winter bouquets. Grows well at seashore. In the language of flowers: "Your wish will come true."

124. HEATHER
(*Calluna vulgaris*)

Height: to 3 ft.
Evergreen
Season of Flowering: Summer, Fall
Colorful
Location: full sun, light shade
Soil: acid, light sandy
Propagation: soft and hardwood cuttings.
Zone 5

Rosy-purple bell-shaped flowers crowd the upright branching stems. Foliage silver-gray, pinkish-bronze. The famed Scotch heather of Highland Moors. Mulch with leaf mold, peat, or pine needles.

125. HOLLY, CALIFORNIA
(*Heteromeles arbutifolia*)

Height: to 15–25 ft.
Evergreen
Season of Flowering: Summer
Fruit
Location: full sun
Soil: rich loam
Propagation: seed
Zone 9

Small, many-branched tree. Thick, glossy leaves and delicate, white flowers. Clusters of bright red berries make fine holiday decorations. Give good drainage and full sun.

126. HONEYSUCKLE, BOX
(*Lonicera nitida*)

Height: to 5 ft.
Evergreen
Season of Flowering: Summer
Fragrant
Location: full sun
Soil: rich loam
Propagation: softwood cuttings
Zone 7

Fine for a bank cover, a clipped or natural hedge, or foundation planting. Compact shrub with lustrous leaves, and fragrant creamy white flowers. Prune to keep in shape.

127. HYDRANGEA, SMOOTH
(*Hydrangea arborescens 'grandiflora'*)

Height: to 4 ft.
Deciduous
Season of Flowering: Summer
Location: full sun, light shade
Soil: rich loam
Propagation: soft and hardwood cuttings
Zone 4

Flat clusters of white flowers remain in bloom many weeks. Southern mountaineers made a healing medicine from the peeled-off bark (of which there are several layers).

128. HYDRANGEA, OAKLEAF
(*Hydrangea quercifolia*)

Height: to 5 ft.
Deciduous
Season of Flowering: Summer
Colorful foliage
Location: full sun, light shade
Soil: rich loam
Propagation: soft and hardwood cuttings
Zone 5

Myriads of panicles of white flowers mature to rose. Protect from the North wind. If the tops winter kill, trim back and a new bush grows. Masses of rich green oak-like leaves turn purple in fall.

129. JACARANDA
(Jacaranda mimosafolia)

Height: to 50 ft.
Evergreen
Season of Flowering: Summer
Location: full sun, light shade
Soil: average
Propagation: softwood cuttings, seed
Zone 10

Spectacular clouds of violet-blue blooms and lacy foliage. Thrives in areas of prolonged droughts. Grows in Central and South America. Falling flowers attractively carpet ground beneath, remaining fresh for days.

130. LEATHERWOOD
(Cyrilla racemiflora)

Height: 5–10 ft.
Deciduous in North, Evergreen in South
Season of Flowering: Summer
Colorful foliage
Location: light shade
Propagation: root cuttings, softwood cuttings
Zone 6

Named because the twigs and stems are flexible. Flowers are small and white. Shiny leaves turn bright orange in August.

131. LILAC, JAPANESE TREE
(Syringa reticulata)

Height: to 30 ft.
Evergreen
Season of Flowering: Summer
Location: full sun
Soil: average
Propagation: softwood cuttings
Zone 4

Native to Japan. Beautiful white flowers open in large, loose panicles. Very appealing reddish-gray smooth bark. Blossoms have a bad smell but worth growing for their loveliness. Remove faded blooms for best display next year.

132. MOUNTAIN-LAUREL; CALICO BUSH
(*Kalmia latifolia*)

Height: to 10 ft.
Evergreen
Season of Flowering: Summer
Location: light shade
Soil: acid, rich loam
Propagation: seed
Zone 4

Deep, pink buds open to pale, pink flowers. Thrives naturalized, and is especially compatible growing under oaks. If plant becomes leggy, prune drastically and it grows up solid and compact again. Called "Spoon wood" by Indians who carved utensils out of it.

133. MOUNTAIN-LAUREL
(*Kalmia polifolia*)

Height: to 3 ft.
Evergreen
Season of Flowering: Summer
Location: full sun, light shade
Soil: acid
Propagation: hardwood cuttings, seeds
Zone 2

Grows wild in bogs across North America. Appealing rosy-purple flowers. Shiny evergreen leaves. Easy if grown in acid moist peaty soil. Mulch with oak leaves.

134. NANDINA
(*Nandina domestica*)

Height: to 8 ft.
Deciduous in North, Evergreen in South
Season of Flowering: Summer
Colorful foliage and fruit
Location: full sun, light shade
Soil: rich loam
Propagation: softwood cuttings, seed
Zones 6, 7

Small white flowers, followed by tight clusters of bright red fruit. In China if marital discord occurs each goes separately and tells it all to the Nandina. Harmony is restored! Hence called "Domestica." When bush is as large as you want, cut ⅓ of canes choosing oldest ones at ground. This keeps it compact.

135. OCEAN SPRAY
(*Holodiscus discolor*)

Height: to 12 ft.
Deciduous
Season of Flowering: Summer
Location: full sun, light shade
Soil: rich loam
Propagation: softwood cuttings, seed
Zone 5

Creamy white feathery flowers in loose clusters like blowing seafoam. Undersides of foilage silvery-gray and slightly downy. Remove faded blossoms.

136. OLIVE, RUSSIAN
(*Elaeagnus angustifolia*)

Height: to 20 ft.
Deciduous
Season of Flowering: Summer
Fruit
Fragrant
Location: full sun
Soil: average
Propagation: seed
Zone 2

Handsome silver-gray foliage grows in irregular and picturesque shapes. Yellow berries covered with silvery scales come in late summer. Thrives in dry areas.

137. PEARLEAF; BIRD'S EYE BUSH
(*Ochna serrulata*)

Height: to 6 ft.
Evergreen
Season of Flowering: Summer
Fruit
Colorful
Location: full sun, light shade
Soil: average
Propagation: seed
Zone 10

From Africa. Interesting all year. In spring leaves turn bronze, masses of yellow flowers appear in summer, jet black berries are set on bright red cushions in autumn.

138. POMEGRANATE
(*Punica granatum*)

Height: to 12 ft.
Deciduous
Season of Flowering: Summer
Fruit
Location: full sun
Soil: average
Propagation: softwood cuttings, seed
Zone 8

Scarlet flowers with white striped petals bloom for weeks. Grow protected by a west wall. Tree-ripened fruit delicious in salads and plain.

139. PRIVET, BORDER
(*Ligustrum obtusifolium*)

Height: to 10 ft.
Deciduous
Season of Flowering: Summer
Fragrant
Location: full sun
Soil: average
Propagation: softwood cuttings, seed
Zone 3

Grow as a hedge or a spreading arching shrub. Prolific white flowers in nodding clusters. Small black fruit. Tough and hardy. Thrives north to Montreal and Quebec.

140. PRIVET, COMMON
(*Ligustrum vulgare*)

Height: to 15 ft.
Deciduous in North, Evergreen in South
Season of Flowering: Summer
Fruit
Location: full sun, light shade
Soil: average
Propagation: softwood cuttings, seed
Zone 4

One of the best hedge plants. Trim as a hedge to 6 feet, or grow as a loose shrub. Attractive white flowers, small black fruits. Spring cuttings readily root in a shady area for new plants. Thrives at the seashore.

141. RHODODENDRON; ROSEBAY
(*Rhododendron maximum*)

Height: to 20 ft.
Evergreen
Season of Flowering: Summer
Location: light shade, no sun
Soil: acid, rich loam
Propagation: hardwood cuttings
Zone 3

Native to forests from Nova Scotia to Georgia. Makes an excellent screen planting. Flowers in large clusters open rose to purple-pink. Water in dry weather. Give plenty of humus.

142. ROCK-ROSE
(*Cistus x hybridus*)

Height: to 3 ft.
Deciduous
Season of Flowering: Summer
Location: full sun
Soil: light sandy, alkaline
Propagation: seed
Zone 8

Flowers with crinkled petals. Blooms for weeks. Thrives in poor soil and drought, on hot banks, in sandy land or desert or at the seashore. Grows in southern California.

143. ROSE, CABBAGE
(*Rosa centifolia*)

Height: to 6 ft.
Deciduous
Season of Flowering: Summer
Fruit
Fragrant
Location: full sun, light shade
Soil: average
Propagation: softwood cuttings
Zone 5

Old-fashioned cabbage rose. Thorny bushes with graceful sweeping branches. Fragrant pink, white, dark red double flowers. Resists drought and wind and adapts to poor soil. Fall fruits attract birds.

144. ROSE, EGLANTINE
(*Rosa eglanteria*)

Height: to 6 ft.
Deciduous
Season of Flowering: Summer
Fruit
Fragrance, flowers and foliage
Location: full sun, light shade
Soil: average
Propagation: softwood cuttings
Zone 7

The Sweet Briar rose. Small white and pink flowers cover the bush. Blossoms sweet-scented, and the foliage has the fragrance of ripe apples. May be clipped into hedge or planted as separate bushes. Prune to shape in early spring. Easy to grow.

145. ROSE, RUGOSE
(*Rosa rugosa*)

Height: to 6 ft.
Deciduous
Season of Flowering: Summer
Fruit
Fragrant
Location: full sun
Soil: adaptable
Propagation: softwood cuttings
Zone 2

Originally from the Orient. Grows wild at the shore and often in pure sand. Survives drought. Single flowers, pink, white, red. Extremely fragrant. Large round fall "hips" are most attractive to look at. They also make delicious jam (if not sprayed) which is high in vitamin C.

146. ROSE OF SHARON
(*Hibiscus syriacus*)

Height: to 12 ft.
Deciduous
Season of Flowering: Summer
Location: full sun
Soil: average
Propagation: softwood cuttings
Zone 4

Pink, white, red, blue single and double flowers. Large saucer-shaped blossoms float indoors in a bowl, fresh for days. Attract bees and butterflies. Plant with manure and compost. Water in drought.

147. ST. JOHNSWORT
(*Hypericum kalmianum*)

Height: to 3 ft.
Deciduous
Season of Flowering: Summer, Fall
Fragrant
Location: full sun
Soil: adaptable
Propagation: softwood cuttings
Zone 3

Low mounded bush covered with bright yellow cup-shaped flowers. Tolerates hot, dry, sunny, sandy soil. Prune in early spring to keep shapely and compact.

148. SILKTREE
(*Albizia julibrissin*)

Height: to 30 ft.
Deciduous in North, Evergreen in South
Season of Flowering: Summer
Location: full sun
Soil: adaptable
Propagation: root cuttings, seed
Zone 7

Deep green feathery foliage covered with fluffy pink flowers. Adapts to most soils. Hardy to zero degrees. A pink snow when stamens fall.

149. SMOKE-TREE
(*Cotinus coggygria*)

Height: to 15 ft.
Deciduous
Season of Flowering: Summer
Colorful
Location: full sun
Soil: average
Propagation: seed
Zone 5

A spreading shrub whose flower stalks develop long hairs and become feathery, providing a smoky appearance. Goes through a color cycle: first chartreuse, next dull purple and in fall it turns bright orange.

150. SNOWBELL, JAPANESE
(*Styrax japonica*)

Height: to 20 ft.
Deciduous
Season of Flowering: Summer
Fruit
Fragrance
Location: full sun, light shade
Soil: acid, rich loam
Propagation: seed, softwood cuttings
Zone 5

Slow growing tree covered in early summer with drooping bell-like white flowers. The fruit like tiny footballs is decorative in fall indoor arrangements. Protect from wind. Give ample space.

151. SNOWBERRY
(*Symphoricarpos albus*)

Height: to 4 ft.
Deciduous
Season of Flowering: Summer, Fall
Fruit
Location: light shade, no sun
Soil: average
Propagation: softwood cuttings
Zone 4

An arching shrub producing large white berries for several weeks in the fall. Pink bell-shaped summer flowers. Thrives in shade. Feed lime, likes clay soil.

152. SOURWOOD
(*Oxydendrum arboreum*)

Height: to 30 ft.
Deciduous
Season of Flowering: Summer, Fall
Colorful
Fragrant
Location: full sun, no sun
Soil: acid, rich loam
Propagation: seed, division
Zone 4

Slender tree with twisting trunk and glossy leaves. Drooping clusters of small, waxy bell-shaped florets at the top of the tree dust the foliage white for six weeks or more. Lives 100 years. Sourwood honey especially prized in North Carolina and Tennessee mountains. Dramatic scarlet autumn foliage lasts a month or more.

153. SPIRAEA
(*Spiraea bumalda* 'Anthony Waterer')

Height: to 2 ft.
Deciduous
Season of Flowering: Summer
Fragrant
Location: full sun
Soil: average
Propagation: softwood cuttings
Zone 4

Flat-headed crimson flowers with meadowsweet fragrance. Makes splendid indoor bouquets. Extremely hardy in cold climates. Grows to 5° below zero. Easy, bright, and gay.

154. STARBUSH
(*Turraea obtusifolia*)

Height: to 3 ft.
Deciduous
Season of Flowering: Summer, Fall
Fragrant
Location: light shade
Soil: average
Propagation: seed
Zone 9

Compact shrub covered with deep green foliage sprinkled with white starry blossoms. Jasmine-like perfume. Must have perfect drainage. Use sprays for party decorations and the whole room will be filled with their exotic tropical fragrance.

155. STEPHANANDRA, CUT-LEAF
(*Stephanandra incisa*)

Height: to 5 ft.
Deciduous
Season of Flowering: Summer
Colorful fall foliage
Location: light shade, no sun
Soil: rich loam
Propagation: softwood cuttings, division of
   clumps
Zone 5

Native to Korea, Japan, this shrub brings a touch of the Orient. Innumerable white flowers starry at branch tips. Very easy to grow. Interesting the year round with purple fall leaves and attractive brown-tinted winter branches.

156. STEWARTIA
(*Stewartia malacodendron*)

Height: to 12 ft.
Deciduous
Season of Flowering: Summer
Colorful in autumn
Fragrant
Location: full sun, light shade
Soil: rich loam
Propagation: seed
Zone 7

White cup-like flowers with golden anthers. Bark flakes off causing interesting patterns on branches. Leaves orange in autumn. Water in drought. Add compost when planting. Give winter protection.

157. STRAWBERRY TREE
(*Arbutus unedo*)

Height: to 30 ft.
Evergreen
Season of Flowering: Summer
Fruit: colorful fall berries
Location: full sun
Soil: rich loam
Propagation: seed
Zone 8

Originally from the Mediterranean Sea. Beautiful and versatile: may be used in a shrub border, as a hedge, or a small specimen tree. Lustrous dark green leaves. Small pink or white flowers in drooping panicles. Bright red fall berries.

158. SUMMERSWEET; SWEET PEPPERBUSH
(*Clethra alnifolia*)

Height: to 10 ft.
Deciduous
Season of Flowering: Summer
Colorful fall foliage
Location: full sun, light shade
Soil: acid, rich loam
Propagation: softwood cuttings, seed
Zone 4

Innumerable upright spikes of white flowers that cover the bush are spicy and fragrant, especially at night. Lasts well in house. The foliage dazzling yellow in autumn. Water in drought. Grows in swamps and bordering small lakes near the coast.

159. SWEETSPIRE
(*Itea virginica*)

Height: to 6 ft.
Deciduous
Season of Flowering: Summer
Colorful fall leaves
Fragrant
Location: full sun, light shade
Soil: rich loam
Propagation: softwood cuttings
Zone 6

Small fragrant white flowers string along the branches. Bright red fall foliage. A rare shrub and seldom seen in home gardens. Likes moist areas near streams but adapts to drier spots. Sturdy.

160. VIBURNUM; FRAGRANT SNOWBALL
(*Viburnum* x *carlcephalum*)

Height: to 8 ft.
Deciduous
Season of Flowering: Summer
Fragrant
Location: light shade
Soil: rich loam
Propagation: softwood cuttings
Zone 5

Originated in England, introduced here recently, Compact shrub. Large six-inch fragrant flower clusters. Brilliant autumn foliage. Benefits from mulch of leaves.

Fall Flowering

161. CLOVER, BUSH
(*Lespedeza thunbergii*)

Height: to 4 ft.
Deciduous
Season of Flowering: Fall
Location: full sun
Soil: light sandy
Propagation: softwood cuttings
Zone 6

Arching willowy stems. Pinkish lavender flowers resembling peas, trail in clusters at branch tips. Thrives in dry sandy soil. To keep compact and shapely, cut to ground each spring.

162. ELSHOLTZIA
(*Elsholtzia stauntonii*)

Height: 2–5 ft.
Deciduous
Season of Flowering: Fall
Fragrant
Location: full sun
Soil: average
Propagation: softwood cuttings, seed
Zone 4

Grows taller in warmer climates. Spikes of lavender pink flowers. The light green leaves are aromatic when crushed. Grow in a bed with chrysanthemums for a delightful combination. To keep compact and bushy, cut to ground each spring.

163. WITCH-HAZEL
(*Hamamelis virginiana*)

Height: to 15 ft.
Deciduous
Season of Flowering: Fall
Colorful fall leaves
Fragrant
Location: full sun, light shade
Soil: average
Propagation: seed
Zone 4

Charming yellow fall flowers tumble over the branches, each like a tangled skein of gold embroidery thread. Exudes a dusky sweet spicy scent. Grows in swampy areas. Witch-hazel made from bark and leaves. Bright yellow fall foliage.

Winter Flowering

164. ACACIA
(*Acacia baileyana*)

Height: to 30 ft.
Evergreen
Season of Flowering: Winter, Spring
Fragrant
Location: full sun, light shade
Soil: average
Propagation: softwood cuttings, seed
Zone 10

Blue-green lacy foliage hidden in late winter beneath tossing sprays of fragrant golden flowers. Thrives in semi-drought areas of South and Southwest. Sometimes called Cootamundra-Wattle.

165. CAMELLIA
(*Camellia japonica*)

Height: 6–15 ft.
Evergreen
Season of Flowering: Winter
Location: light shade
Soil: acid, rich loam
Propagation: softwood cuttings, seed
Zone 7

Red, rose, pink, white waxy petalled flowers come both single and double and bloom for months in between cold spells. Mulch with old leaves. Grows further north if protected. In the language of flowers: "I shall love you always."

166. CAMELLIA
(*Camellia sasanqua*)

Height: to 12 ft.
Evergreen
Season of Flowering: Winter
Location: light shade, full sun
Soil: acid, rich loam
Propagation: softwood cuttings, seed
Zone 7

Light red markings on white-petalled flower. No two blooms variegated in same pattern. Sometimes pure white, pink, double or single blooms. Feed cottonseed meal and acid plant food. Give peaty soil, leaf mold. Old time symbol of steadfastness. Blooms all fall until Christmas.

167. DAPHNE
(*Daphne mezereum*)

Height: to 3 ft.
Deciduous
Season of Flowering: Winter, Spring
Fruit: fragrant
Location: full sun
Soil: acid
Propagation: hardwood and softwood cuttings,
    root cuttings, seed
Zone 5

Fragrant rosy pink flowers unfold in winter in south, in spring in north. Scarlet fruits close to the branches in fall. Protect on north and west.

168. JASMINE, WINTER
(*Jasminum nudiflorum*)

Height: to 4 ft.; sprawls, trails
Deciduous
Season of Flowering: Winter
Fragrant
Location: full sun, light shade
Soil: acid
Propagation: cover trailing branch with dirt,
    new plant forms
Zone 7

Large and scrawly thickets over the southern countryside thrive, tumble over stone walls. Gay sweet-scented golden flowers unfold off and on for months. Stems green all winter. May be an espalier. Fine for forcing indoors. Old-time symbol of timidity and modesty.

169. POINSETTIA
(*Euphorbia pulcherrima*)

Height: 10 ft.
Deciduous
Season of Flowering: Winter
Location: full sun
Soil: rich loam
Propagation: softwood cuttings
Zone 9

Leggy shoots crowned with bright red bracts for the holidays and many weeks beyond. Cut stalks back drastically after blossoms fade, water through winter and set in the garden through the summer. Will bloom year after year.

Bibliography

A Herbal of All Sorts—Geoffrey Grigson

The Book of Shrubs—Alfred C. Hottes

The Concise Encyclopedia of Favorite Flowering Shrubs—
Marjorie J. Dietz

Field Book of American Trees and Shrubs—F. Schuyler
Mathews

Folklore and Symbolism of Flowers, Plants and Trees—Ernst
and Johanna Lehner

The Fragrant Path—Louise Beebe Wilder

Garden Plants in Color—Edited By Henry J. Skinner

Gray's Manual of Botany—M. L. Fernald

Hortus Second—Compiled by L. H. Bailey and Ethel Zoe Bailey

The Legends of Flowers—Mrs. Alexander Kennedy

Shrubs and Trees for the Home Landscape—James Bush-Brown

Shrubs in the Garden—Vernon Quinn

Stalking the Wild Asparagus—Euell Gibbons

Index

Abelia, Glossy, 49
Abelia grandiflora, 49
Abelia-Leaf, Korean, 11
Abeliophyllum distichum, 11
Almond, Flowering, 11
Acacia, 73
Acacia, Rose, 49
Acacia baileyana, 73
Aesculus parviflora, 50
Albizia julibrissin, 63
Amelanchier grandiflora, 39
Andromeda, 11
Apricot, 12
Arbutus unedo, 66
Aronia arbutifolia, 17
Asiatic Sweetleaf, 39
Azalea, Chinese, 12; Japanese, 12; Korean, 13; Pinxter, 13; White Swamp, 49

Barberry, 13
Barberry, Common, 14
Bauhinia variegata, 31
Beach Plum, 14
Beauty Bush, 50
Berberis thunbergii, 13; *vulgaris*, 14
Bird's Eye Bush, 59
Blueberry, Highbush, 14
Blue-Spiraea, 50
Bridalwreath, 41
Broom, Scotch, 15; Warminster, 15
Buckeye Bottlebrush, 50
Buddleia alternifolia, 15; *davidi*, 51
Butterfly Bush, 51
Butterfly-Bush, Fountain, 15

Calico Bush, 58
California-Lilac, 16
Callicarpa dichotoma, 26
Calluna vulgaris, 55
Calycanthus floridus, 42
Camellia, 73
Camellia japonica, 73; *sasanqua*, 73
Caryopteris incana, 50
Ceanothus purpureus, 16
Cercis canadensis, 37

Chaenomeles speciosa, 36; *speciosa lagenaria*, 37
Cherry, Double White Flowering, 16; Weeping, 17; Yoshino, 17
Cherry-Laurel, 16
Chimonanthus praecox, 45; *virginicus*, 53
Chokeberry, Red, 17
Choisya ternata, 29
Cinquefoil Bush, 51
Cinquefoil, Shrubby, 39
Cistus hybridus, 61
Clerodendrum trichotomum, 54
Clethra alnifolia, 66
Clover, Bush, 71
Cornelian Cherry, 18
Cornus florida, 21; *florida rubra*, 21; *kousa*, 52; *mas*, 18
Corylus americana, 24; *sinensis*, 44
Cotinus coggygria, 63
Cotoneaster, Rock, 18
Cotoneaster horizontalis, 18
Crabapple, Bechtel, 18; Kaido, 19; Sargent, 19; Showy, 19
Crape Myrtle, 51
Crataegus oxyacantha, 24; *phaenopyrum*, 24
Currant, Flowering, 20
Cyrilla racemiflora, 57
Cytisus praecox, 15; *scoparius*, 15

Daphne, 20, 74
Daphne burkwoodii 'Somerset', 20; *mezereum*, 74
Deutzia gracilis, 20; *lemoine*, 52
Deutzia, Lemoine, 52; Slender, 20
Dogwood, 21; Japanese, 52; Pink, 21

Elaeagnus angustifolia, 59
Elsholtzia, 71
Elsholtzia stauntonii, 71
Enkianthus, 21
Enkianthus campanulatus, 21
Erica cinerea, 55
Euphorbia pulcherrima, 74
Exochorda giraldii, 33; *racemosa*, 33

Firethorn, 22
Forsythia, 22
Forsythia intermedia, 22
Fothergilla, 22
Fothergilla gardeni, 22
Franklin Tree, 53
Franklinia alatamaha, 53
Fringetree, 53
Fuchsia, 53
Fuchsia magellanica, 53

Gardenia, 23
Gardenia jasminoides, 23
Genista, 54
Genista cinerea, 54
Glory-Bower, 54
Golden Chain Tree, 23
Golden Rain Tree, 54

Halesia carolina, 40
Hamamelis virginiana, 71
Harlequin, 54
Hardy-Orange, 23
Hawthorn, 24; English 'Paul's Scarlet', 24
Hazel, American, 24
Heath, Bell, 55
Heather, 55
Heteromeles arbutifolia, 55
Hibiscus syriacus, 62
Holly, California, 55
Holly-Olive, 25
Holodiscus discolor, 59
Honeysuckle, Box, 56; Tatarian, 25
Hydrangea, Oakleaf, 56; Smooth, 56
Hydrangea arborescens grandiflora, 56; *quercifolia*, 56
Hypericum calycinum, 38
Hypericum kalmianum, 63

Itea virginica, 67

Jacaranda, 57
Jacaranda mimosafolia, 57
Jasmine, Winter, 74

Jasminum nudiflorum, 74
Jetbead, 25
Jewel Berry, 26
Judas Tree, 37

Kalmia latifolia, 58; *polifolia*, 58
Kerria, 26
Kerria japonica, 26
Koelreuteria paniculata, 54
Kolkwitzia amabilis, 50

Laburnum watereri, 23
Lagerstroemia indica, 51
Leatherleaf, 28
Leatherwood, 57
Lespedeza thunbergii, 71
Leucothoë, 26
Leucothoë fontanesiana, 26
Ligustrum obtusifolium, 60; *vulgare*,
   60
Lilac, Chinese, 27; Common, 27; Jap-
   anese Tree, 57; Persian, 27
Lindera benzoin, 41
Lonicera nitida, 56; *tatarica*, 25

Magnolia, Saucer, 28; Star, 28
Magnolia soulangeana, 28; *stellata*, 28
Mahonia, 28, 29
Mahonia aquifolium, 29; *bealei*, 28
Malus floribunda, 19; *micromalus*, 19;
   sargentii, 19; *yedoensis plena bech-
   tel*, 18
Mexican-Orange, 29
Mock Orange, 29; Sweet, 30
Morus alba, 30
Mountain-Ash, American, 30
Mountain-Laurel, 58
Mulberry, White, 30

Nandina, 58
Nandina domestica, 58
Nerium oleander, 31
Neviusia alabamensis, 40

Ocean Spray, 59
Ochna serrulata, 59
Oleander, 31
Olive, Russian, 59
Orchid Tree, Purple, 31
Oregon Holly-Grape, 29
Osmanthus delavayi, 25
Oxydendrum arboreum, 64

Paeonia lutea, 33; *suffruticosa*, 34
Parrotia, 31

Parrotia persica, 31
Paulownia imperialis, 32
Paulownia tomentosa, 32
Peach, Double Red Flowering, 32;
   Flowering, 32
Pearleaf, 59
Pearl-Bush, 33
Peony, Tree, 33, 34
Philadelphus coronarius, 30; *lemoinei*,
   29
Photinia, 34
Photinia serrulata, 34
Pieris japonica, 11
Pittosporum, 34
Pittosporum tobira, 34
Plum, Flowering, 35; Purple-Leaf, 36
Poinsettia, 74
Pomegranate, 60
Poncirus trifoliata, 23
Potentilla fruticosa 'Gold Drop', 39;
   fruticosa veitchii, 'Mount Everest',
   51
Privet, Border, 60; Common, 60
Prunus armeniaca, 12; *bliredana*, 35;
   cerasifera 'Pissardi', 36; *cerasifera*
   'Thundercloud', 35; *glandulosa*, 11;
   laurocerasus, 16; *maritima*, 14; *per-
   sica*, 32; *persica* 'Rubroplena', 32;
   serrulata 'Kiku-shidare-Zakura', 17;
   serrulata 'Shirofugen', 16; *triloba*, 35;
   yedoensis 'Akebono', 17
Punica granatum, 60
Pussy Willow, French, 36
Pyracantha coccinea, 22

Quince, Flowering, 36; Japanese, 37

Redbud, Eastern, 37
Rhododendron, 37, 61; Catawba, 38
Rhododendron maximum, 61; *carolin-
   ianum*, 37; *catawbiense*, 38; *fortunei*,
   38; *japonicum*, 12; *molle*, 12; *muc-
   ronulatum*, 13; *nudiflorum*, 13; *vis-
   cosum*, 49
Rhodotypos scandens, 25
Ribes sanguineum, 20
Robinia hispida, 49
Rock-Rose, 61
Rosa centifolia, 61; *eglanteria*, 62; *ru-
   gosa*, 62
Rosebay, 61
Rose, Cabbage, 61; Eglantine, 62; Ru-
   gose, 62
Rose of Sharon, 62

St. Johnswort, 38, 63
Salix caprea, 36
Sapphireberry, 39

Shadblow, 39
Silktree, 63
Silverbell Tree, 40
Skimmia, 40
Skimmia japonica, 40
Smoke-Tree, 63
Snowball, Fragrant, 67
Snowbell, Japanese, 64
Snowberry, 64
Snow-Wreath, 40
Sorbaria aitchisonii, 52
Sorbus americana, 30
Sourwood, 64
Spice Bush, 41
Spiraea, 65; Double, 41; Garland, 41;
   Kashmir, False-, 52; Thunbergii, 42
Spiraea arguta, 41; *bumalda* 'Anthony
   Waterer', 65; *prunifolia*, 41; *thun-
   bergii*, 42
Starbush, 65
Stephanandra, Cut-leaf, 65
Stephanandra incisa, 65
Stewartia, 66
Stewartia malacodendron, 66
Strawberry Tree, 66
Strawberry-Shrub, 42
Styrax japonica, 64
Sweet Pepperbush, 66
Sweet Shrub, 42
Sweetspire, 67
Summersweet, 66
Symphoricarpos albus, 64
Symplocos paniculata, 39
Syringa chinensis, 27; *persica*, 27; *reti-
   culata*, 57; *vulgaris*, 27

Tamarisk, 42
Tamarix parviflora, 42
Turraea obtusifolia, 65

Vaccinium corymbosum, 14
Viburnum, 43, 67; Burkwood's, 43;
   Doublefile, 43; Fragrant, 84
Viburnum burkwoodii, 43; *carlesii*, 44;
   carcephalum, 67; *tomentosum*, 43;
   wrightii, 43

Washington Thorn, 24
Weigela, 44
Weigela florida, 44
Winter-Hazel, Chinese, 44
Wintersweet, 45
Witch-Hazel, 71

Zenobia, Dusty, 45
Zenobia pulverulenta, 45